P9-BEE-571

ANOTHER PART OF THE WOOD

ANOTHER PART OF THE WOOD

BERYL BAINBRIDGE

George Braziller   New York

Published in the United States by George Braziller, Inc. in 1980
First published in this edition 1979
Gerald Duckworth & Co. Ltd.
The Old Piano Factory
43 Goucester, London NW1
Original edition first published by Hutchinson, 1968
This edition rewritten and reset
Copyright © 1968, 1980 by Beryl Bainbridge
All rights reserved.
For information, address the publisher:
George Braziller, Inc.
One Park Avenue
New York City, 10016

Library of Congress Cataloging in Publication Data
Bainbridge, Beryl, 1933–
        Another part of the wood.
        I.   Title.
PZ4.B162An   1980   (PR6052A3195)   823′.914   79–27297
ISBN 0–8076–0965–X

Printed in the United States of America
First Edition

For Lilly and Cecil Todes

1

Balfour, unbearably shy, was waiting for them.

He sat on the gate hunching his shoulders, squinting up into the sunlight as the open car came round the corner and went too fast over the bridge. He watched the car's approach with a fixed smile – too wide, too foolish – listening with eyelids fluttering to the optimistic voice of P.J. Proby loud above the noise of the engine.

George MacFarley had told him to meet the visitors. 'You meet them and I'll make tea,' he had promised. 'Right you are,' Balfour had agreed, and half ran, half walked, down the track to the entrance of the woods, leaving George towering outside the door of the Big House, his scarf wound about his throat, his melancholy eyes regarding the forest below him. The Big House was merely one large room with a kitchen built on at the back and a bedroom at the side. Nailed to that was another room, very small, furnished with two bunk beds and a hanging lamp. This was George's bedroom, where he kept his drawing board, his set-square, some hammers, an axe and two spades. His saw, always greased after use, hung in a sack behind the door. Pinned to the wooden wall beside the bunks was a plan of the woods which George had drawn showing the positioning of the huts and the various species of trees. In the bottom corner were printed the words 'Plan of Nant MacFarley Camp' and then, modestly small,

'George David MacFarley, Flintshire.' The name Nant MacFarley Camp wasn't always used. George's mother referred to the estate as the Family Resting Ground, the haven to which they could retreat when the demands of city life became overwhelming. Most weekends Balfour accompanied the MacFarleys to the Resting Ground – returning to his factory bench on a Monday morning in a state of exhaustion. When there weren't any dead trees to be felled and sawn into logs, there were living ones to be inspected and new ones to be planted. There was drainage to improve and space to be cleared, chemicals to be dug into the soil and fungi to be torn out, paths to be laid, steps to be cut, hinges to be oiled, window frames to be examined for warping. A porch was planned for the entrance of the Big House. Another shed would be erected on the other side of the stream to hold the increasing stores: fluorides and chlorine, acids and caustics, sulphur dioxide, cyanide, methyl alcohol, strychnine, carbon bisulphide, paraffin, calor gas, petroleum, turpentine – the list was as endless as the work to be done. Under the pampered trees and the curving sky the MacFarleys toiled without ceasing. Balfour called it the Labour Camp. Nevertheless he had arranged to spend his summer holiday, his fourteen days away from the factory, at the Camp. Mr and Mrs MacFarley wouldn't be there; they had gone abroad. But Balfour had discovered on arrival that he wasn't going to be alone with George. George had invited friends – a man with a beard called Joseph and somebody named Kidney. What was worse, Joseph had apparently taken it upon himself to ask two other people to stay – people whom George had never met. George said that very possibly Joseph would also bring a woman. He usually did. Balfour could tell that George was none too pleased about the arrangements, though he didn't say much. George never said much.

The car, radio blaring, stopped. Seated beside Joseph was a fair-haired girl, between them a child in a pom-pom hat and in the back a youth with a rosy face. Raindrops slid off the dark blue bonnet, and P.J. Proby still shouted up into the trees, long after the engine had stopped, that somewhere there was a place for them.

Joseph got out of the car and went easily over the mud, thrusting his hand forward and saying 'You must be Balfour. How are things? How's George? Everything under control?'

The child in the car clambered over the edge of the door. He said petulantly, 'Can I have the kite now, Daddy?', and without waiting for an answer began to tug at the handle of the boot.

Joseph, stretching his arms high, said 'Wait a moment, Roland, just wait a moment. Dreadful journey.' He lowered his outflung arms and looked at Balfour, still hunched on the gate. 'I picked up Roland in Liverpool, you know, but I've come all the way from London. Bloody cold, bloody awful journey.'

'George is making tea,' said Balfour, clearing his throat, too shy to look at the girl. 'He thought you could do with a cuppa.'

Joseph noticed his bad complexion and felt sorry for him. He extracted a kite from the boot. The string was red knitting-wool bound round and round a piece of cardboard. 'There's no wind, Roland,' he said. 'Leave it until there's a wind.'

The other passenger had remained where he was in the car. He sat stiffly and stared at the windscreen. 'We had a bad journey,' he said, speaking to no one. 'We had a bad journey.' Looking up, he saw Balfour on the gate and blushed.

'This is Kidney.' Joseph motioned with his hand at the youth in the car.

The child dropped his scarlet wool into the mud and broke out crying. Balfour got down from his perch and lifted the string from the path.

Joseph was moving luggage from the back of the car – some cases, a wicker basket, a long red and black cardboard box. 'Had to bring this. Dotty can't live without her Monopoly,' he said.

Cleaning the kite wool, Balfour nodded, expressing

9

sympathy, he hoped, giving the blonde girl a quick glance. But she was looking at Joseph, with eyes narrowed, and he bent his head again.

'Come on, Kidney.' Joseph addressed the figure in the car severely. 'Stir yourself, boy.'

Stirred, Kidney opened the door of the Jaguar and stepped down. He looked at the ground and shifted his feet. 'It was a bad journey,' he repeated, face flushed and manner intent. Round and contoured like a girl, buttocks vast in his corduroy trousers, he waved fat hands in the summer air. Silently he removed things from the seats of the car.

When the car was finally unpacked, they went in single file through the gate, keeping to the path that climbed upward through the trees. To the right the pines rose to the edge of an unseen field. To the left the ground fell away to the stream in the valley below, hidden among the black poplars and the beech trees. The air hummed with gnats. Mrs MacFarley called the valley the Glen. She called the light at early evening the gloaming. She liked to go Roaming in the Gloaming in the Glen.

They passed a badger's hole at the foot of a tree and a clump of foxgloves lolling in the breeze. 'Don't ever touch one of those,' said Balfour strictly, apparently to the child, manoeuvring himself and the Monopoly box round the swollen purple heads. 'George wants them to seed.'

'Really,' said Joseph, 'Spot of colour, what?' He turned on the path, halting his followers, and spoke to his son. 'You heard what Balfour said, Roland. You mustn't touch the foxgloves. George wants them to seed.'

'George is the biggest man in the world,' sang the child. 'George is a giant. I told them at school. I told them George was a giant.' He jumped anxiously along the track.

'How high is he?' asked Kidney. Behind the bottles of Ribena, he blinked sweat from his eyes.

'Six foot eight, nine,' Joseph said. He leapt athletically over

10

a small boulder, gracefully landing with luggage swinging and beard quivering. 'Quite a size, Kidney.'

Balfour tried to remember what George had told him about Joseph. He was divorced, apparently, from a wife who painted, the administrator of a technical college, living with a woman, presumably Dotty: a man, according to George, given to stimulating talk, a non-conformist. To Balfour, even on such short acquaintance, Joseph seemed the arch-conformer of all time, stereotyped, well-bred, unemotional. Nothing had been said about Kidney.

Joseph put the cases down in the grass and wiped with a handkerchief at the spots of mud drying on the leather of his boots. Dotty looked at him with hostility.

'Must keep up appearances, you know,' Joseph shouted to Balfour. Stooping, he picked up the cases and asked, 'All right, Dot-Dot? Everything all right?' He tried to put an arm about her, a case in his hand, and caught her a blow on the hip, knocking her against him. She scowled, and stepped back to her rightful place, behind Joseph and in front of the blocked Kidney.

'George is making tea in Hut 2,' called Balfour.

'Hut 2, Hut 2,' echoed Joseph, somewhere behind him on the path, which had grown steeper and more waterlogged.

The girl said something then, but her words were inaudible to Balfour, as he hastened up the slope hampered by his self-imposed Monopoly burden. He hoped she hadn't remarked on his acne. One foot after the other, keeping his balance with difficulty on the uneven ground, he strained to reach the summit of the path.

Roland began to sing. He piped shrilly under the dripping trees:

'Bobby Shaftoe's gone to sea,
Silver bottles on his knee ...'

'Buckles, buckles,' corrected his father, trampling mud

11

underfoot, swinging his elegant luggage high above the damp grasses.

'He'll come home and marry me-e,
Bonny Bobby Shaftoe-O.'

'We're there,' Balfour shouted. He jogged thankfully down the home path, heart thudding in his breast.

Hut 2 was made of wood without embellishments of stone or slate: one long room with bunks at the end and an iron stove opposite the door, the kitchen through an opening to the right of the stove. There was a bench outside the hut and two wooden steps at the door. Red curtains hung on either side of the end window. Laid down on the bench outside was a hammer and some nails. From the path the mountain wasn't visible. Nor was George.

Balfour put down his Monopoly box on the scrubbed top of the table and told them apologetically that he couldn't imagine where old George had got to. He went into the kitchen but found it empty, and the kettle empty also, the cups still on their hooks above the sink. 'Must have gone to look at something or other,' he said. He stood in the doorway of the kitchen, resentful that he should be left in such a position, looking at Kidney still outside the hut, arms full of groceries. He was aware that no one save himself felt any embarrassment. The girl had seated herself in the rocking chair by the stove, rugs in a heap on the floor where she had dropped them, arms folded across her chest. Joseph had found a pocket mirror on the shelf. He was holding it cupped in one hand, face twisted as he studied his image.

'I've got another cold sore coming. I can't bear a marked face,' he told Balfour bitterly, dabbing at his erupting skin with his mud-stained handkerchief.

Balfour, only partly shielded by the doorway of the kitchen, raised an arm to cover his blemished complexion but dropped it again: after all, he couldn't spend the next six days with his face hidden. Though the journey from the entrance of the woods to Hut 2 hadn't been a noticeably merry one, he was conscious that the visitors' spirits had fallen.

Roland came in from his search for George and flung himself against the rocking chair, pushing his head, still in its pom-pom hat, against the girl's face. 'Why don't we do something?' he asked. Already he was bored.

His father glanced once about the room and yawned loudly, thinking of all the preparation: the denim outfit bought to make Dotty feel secure, the choice selection of paperbacks, the sheets freshly laundered, Roland's kite, all the business of stopping the milk and leaving the caged bird with the people downstairs. Now that they were here, it was as he had suspected: nowhere was either better or worse than anywhere else. Most of all he thought of his good intentions. He shrugged his shoulders, trying to rid himself of dejection, looking at the girl fondling the child's cheek. Making a determined effort for Roland – for Dotty, for himself – he said, 'Well, troops. Action stations. We better get settled in.'

'You're in Hut 4 on the other side of the stream,' mumbled Balfour. But Joseph was already nodding his head in a businesslike way, picking up rugs and cases in readiness for departure. 'Come along, Dot-Dot. Mustn't be lazy.'

'I don't think I'll bother, if it's all the same to you. You go and get settled in and I'll wait here for you.' Deliberately she leaned her head against the back of the rocking-chair and closed her eyes.

Without further comment Joseph left the hut, passing Kidney on the path. Meekly, unquestioningly, the youth turned about, chin down to the edge of his load, and followed him. Lastly Roland ran out of the door, leaving Balfour alone in the hut with Dotty. For a moment he stood where he was, waiting to see if she would speak to him; but she didn't, so he sought refuge in the kitchen, willing George to return and deliver him. As he ran water into the tin kettle a spider moved across the bottom of the sink. He removed the lid from the kettle and slopped water against the animal. Dismayed at its clinging persistence, he put down the kettle on the draining board and with the edge of the washing-up bowl rammed the spider into the plug hole and turned the tap violently.

When Joseph reached the stream at the bottom of the valley, Roland immediately wanted his red boat to sail in the water. After an argument, Joseph unzipped the bag handed to him by his ex-wife in Liverpool and ferreted out the required toy.

With instructions as to how to find Hut 4 and how not to fall in the water, he and Kidney continued their climb up the path and left the child to play. With only Kidney to care for, Joseph withdrew into himself and strode up the rough slope, yawning repeatedly. At the hut he kicked open the door with his foot and put his cases down on the floor, instructing Kidney where to put the grocery box and the wicker basket, in a voice perfectly polite, his body active and his mind empty of everything save the business of settling in. Expertly and tidily he laid out the luggage and snapping the locks of the pigskin cases told Kidney to unpack his clothing.

The youth began slowly to do as he was told. He laid his pullover down on the narrow settee and stared at it. Empty of him and newly washed, it looked too small. His mother had knitted it some part of every night for almost three winter months. Occasionally the ball of wool had fallen from her knee and rolled away under the sofa and then he had gone down on hands and knees to retrieve it for her. He would press his head sideways against the frill of the sofa and let his hand crawl in the darkness over the soft pile of the carpet. Grunting with exertion, he would place the wool back on his mother's lap and sit again in the armchair, hands still curved. The nights his mother had gone out to her bridge, or to cocktail parties with his father, the knitting lay pierced by its steel skewers on the top of the television set. He had looked at the pictures moving on the screen and up at the woollen shape, and sometimes it seemed as if the flickering images were just an extension of the needles flashing and his pullover was growing

14

without his mother's help. When the compulsion to touch became too strong, he would go upstairs to the bathroom and clean his teeth. Once he hadn't been able to and had pulled at the knitting needles. Under his fingers the stitches began to dissolve away. His mother was angry and threatened never to finish his present, so he stopped watching television the nights she went out. At Christmas when he had unwrapped it from the patterned paper he had felt only disappointment at its fat completion. Here in the hut with Joseph he began to feel protective towards it again. He folded the pullover carefully. Once he glanced up to see if Joseph was watching him. When he saw he wasn't, his eyes filled with tears. Frowning, he tied the arms in a knot and bundled it into a drawer.

'Not that drawer,' said Joseph. He rose and strode over to the chest of drawers, pulled out the offending jumper and threw it back on to the settee. Bending down to finish his unpacking of the wicker basket, he said by way of explanation: 'That drawer is for Roland. Next to mine. Me and Roland together. Get the idea? Anyway, that's no way to treat your clothes. Fold it properly.'

'Sorry,' mumbled Kidney with effort, and sat down heavily on the sofa.

Joseph turned to look at Kidney. 'Do you want to know where the lavatory is?'

'Yes, please.'

'Down the path and through the trees.'

Joseph got up from his unpacking and taking Kidney's arm guided him to the door. 'Down that way,' he explained again patiently, pointing along the mud path.

'Down that way,' repeated Kidney. The width of his trousers so extreme that his limbs floundered in corduroy, he rolled walrus-fashion along the path.

Joseph stayed framed in the doorway, gazing before and around him – at the wet field, the slope of damp grass, the thread of path disappearing under the trees. Out of a brown field rose the mountain, partially obscured by mist.

Tomorrow, he promised himself, he would take Roland by the hand and together they would climb to the summit and explore the tower. He would make it like an adventure for the boy, like a challenge, like a prologue to all the bigger and better adventures that they would have one day, like a stepping stone to the real mountains, capped with snow, that they would surely climb. It would be a beginning. He tried to imagine a grown Roland in a man-sized anorak, and failed. His wife had told him not to take a girl along with him. How had she put it? ... 'Try to be alone with Roland for once and leave your bloody women behind.' He studied the mountain beyond the trees. Of course it was really more of a large hill, but it would do for a start, and Roland was only seven. Or was it eight? He felt suddenly depressed at the thought of how easily Roland tired, how his clear treble voice asking intelligent questions could degenerate into a whining request to be carried. Their outing in the end could be a disaster and not a triumph.

The mountain, he realised, looked not unlike Kidney in shape. Why did he find it so difficult to like someone so fleshily built — or too thin, or too small, or too old? Why was it so difficult to like anyone for any length of time, let alone love them? He wasn't sure if he was unable to love because he had no tenderness for himself or because he felt himself to be perfect and out of reach of compassion. His ex-wife said it was because he was a selfish bastard, but that was the same thing. She talked a lot of words about love entering and making one grow and how his particular soul was too small to allow anybody entrance. Possibly she hadn't always thought he had a small soul. His memory of his marriage, of his whole relationship with his wife, was so frail that he couldn't remember for certain why it was they had separated or how long they had been apart, or the duration of their time together. But then he didn't remember either the lengths or the depths of any of his involvements with any one person. He was either absorbed or empty, and one feeling followed the other.

He thought he remembered his wife when they were first married, the girl in the long nightgown with a sleepy face, broad bare feet going over the blind school matting – not going away from him but towards him. He did remember that. He did remember some things. She was always coming towards him, it seemed, mouth shaping his name, a low-pitched droning sound, full of meaning and heavy with love, the sound of a bee making for the hive. When they ate a meal she held his hand or laid her fingers on his knee or leant her head against his shoulder. When he turned his shoulder her hair clung to the cloth of his jacket; if he removed his hands from hers on some pretext, she looked at him with unbearable reproach and laid her damp rejected palm down in her lap and bowed her head. Recovering, but denied bodily contact, she would imprison him by the strength of expression in her eyes. He was forever trying to extricate himself from her touch, her glance, the sound of her voice, all charged with love, sticky as honey, clinging, like the strands of her hair, to the surface of his life. In bed she had swung her pulpy thigh across him and laid her mouth to his breast as if to tear out his heart. When she was pregnant and couldn't sleep, they had gone for walks along the streets late at night; no doubt he had held her hand. She had cried a lot, wept over the deficiency in him, over not getting the response that she craved, the safety she wanted, at being cheated out of her love. He had felt it wasn't him she loved at all, that it was some anonymous love-source that she believed existed within him and was determined to rip out of him at all costs. If he bled in the process that was of no account.

His ex-wife had grown fat now. Kidney wasn't really fat, at least not depressingly white and trembly; but he was feminine in shape and perhaps his whole problem was one of bulk and excess of tissue and nothing at all to do with a trauma over his mother. Perhaps all that had to be done was to dissolve the inhibiting flesh and release the prisoner within. Maybe Kidney would then emerge to function normally, even though

17

there wouldn't be anyone waiting for him outside. He must insist that Kidney do some hard physical exercise and see if it made any difference.

Tomorrow without fail he and Roland would climb that mountain. Believing it, Joseph looked for a moment longer at the forest, at the pattern of light and shade on the mud path before going back inside the hut to finish his unpacking.

In Hut 2 Balfour was watching Dotty. She was leaning against the double-tiered bunks at the end of the hut, her arms stretched wide in a crucified position. Behind her head, the red curtains, crushed by the mattress, framed a view of trees. First there were only leaves; and then beyond, part of a trunk, and further still, proportioned by distance, a whole tree, a mountain ash with arms held out as if in mimicry of the interior girl. Supported by the bunks she moved her arm, and unbuttoning the breast pocket of her denim jacket withdrew an oblong of tobacco in a silver wrapping and a red fold of cigarette papers. Turning round now to face the window, she laid them down on the bed and hunched her shoulders.

Balfour himself didn't smoke, but he watched her bent head and imagined her hands pushing the mahogany grains along the line of thin paper and her pink tongue flicking out to wet and seal the cylindrical fold. She looked as if she could be weeping, crouched over the side of the bunk bed, a line of hair, yellow as butter, fringing the collar of her jacket.

To Balfour it seemed as if they had all been in the hut for years and years and never spoken, he on his stool and George, returned without apology or explanation, seated on the rough bench by the stove, forearm balanced on his knee. Wrapped round the thick column of George's neck was a woollen scarf that fell in equal lengths between his knees and touched the floor and folded once, twice, in knitted bands of maroon and black. As always, he managed to convey both serenity and imbecility at one and the same time – the first by the purity of

18

his limpid eyes now turned towards Balfour, and the other by the curious looseness of his never-ending legs anchored to the floor of the hut by his monstrous army boots.

Dotty left the bunk bed and moved between the two men. She held her cigarette aloft in one hand and with the other touched the lid of the stove.

'Is this thing lit?' she asked. Without waiting for a reply she bent at the waist, and putting one end of the cigarette to her mouth and the other against the surface of the iron stove attempted to draw heat. She tried several times, making little sucking noises, until George said, 'No, it's not lit.'

She stood then, hopeless, the fold of unlit paper clinging to her dry upper lip. 'Matches,' she said, and looked directly at Balfour, who got up at once and fetched them.

'Better let me keep these,' she told Balfour, taking the matches from him. 'I use an awful lot of matches and I do get jumpy if I don't get a light.'

Her cigarette now glowing, she seemed fatter and happier.

She tapped George on the shoulder and asked brightly, 'Don't you ever light the stove?'

'At night.' George shifted his boots about and looked in the direction of the open door. 'Only at night. At night one needs the stove. We shut that door and the kitchen door, and we light the lamps and we all sit round the lit stove.'

'What else do you do?' Dotty inquired.

'We talk or we draw,' said George. Sometimes we go down to the pub in the village, and we discuss things.'

'I don't do any drawing,' said Balfour abruptly, sweat accumulating under his armpits. He hated to be associated with George and his artistic evenings round the stove.

'We're going to play Monopoly, though,' Dotty said. 'I've brought my Monopoly set. We play every night at home, every blessed night. Well, sometimes. Me and Joseph and Kidney.'

Balfour couldn't imagine what home might be like, but he could visualise a table and three chairs grouped about it, and

19

on the chairs the pudsey Kidney with rosy cheeks and the debonair Joseph, dressed maybe in a silk dressing-gown, and Dotty rolling her cigarettes. All of them playing Monopoly.

'Of course, Kidney doesn't really play,' Dotty said, finding herself at the window, viewing the trees and the path empty of Joseph. 'But he tries, and Joseph tries to teach him, though lately he's lost patience.'

'Is he a relation?' asked George.

'No,' said Dotty. 'But you know what Joseph's like – he thinks he's God. Kidney was referred to the college by some clinic or other. To do pottery. Joseph just happened to see him in the canteen. He's got it into his head that there's nothing wrong with Kidney.'

'And is there?' asked George.

'Well, he's certainly thick or something,' Dotty said. 'There was a change at first,' she added grudgingly. 'When Joseph first took him over. He got him to come and live at the flat. He played music to him, read poetry, talked a load of rubbish to him. Kidney really seemed to respond ... at first. He even began to play chess.'

'Chess,' interrupted George, stamping his boots and nodding his head with pleasure.

Dotty wasn't to be checked, by chess or by George. She wasn't so much telling Kidney's story as her own. 'But Joseph always makes the same mistake, every single time. He bought Kidney a book of poems by Donne, with a silly message inside – To My Friend. It was supposed to be meaningful and it meant sweet fanny-all really.' Her voice was uneven, but her face was turned from Balfour and George and it was difficult to tell if it contained anger or grief. 'I mean, he's bought the same book for so many people at one time or another, with the appropriate inscription inside – To My Friend, or My Wife or My Love – and it's a shame really because they're nice poems and you can't even look at them after Joseph has finished with you. Every gesture he makes is just a monotonous repeat of a gesture he's made somewhere else. You see, Kidney really

20

thought Joseph was interested in him. Really thought he cared.' She stopped talking. She wasn't thinking of Kidney at all.

For a time Roland played with his boat in the stream. It was a lovely colour, his red boat, bobbing up and down. He moved his bare feet roughly to slap small waves against its sides and it still rode the water. He didn't care for the feel of the wet mud beneath the soles of his feet and there were sharp things down there, stones and a fragment of glass and a piece of something blue and gold that seemed to move as the water rolled over it. It wasn't a fish and it wasn't a jewel. He would have touched it if he hadn't been alone. Once a strand of wet moss clung to his ankle and he hated that. He put his fingers in the stream and pulled, and it wrapped itself round his wrist like a green bracelet. He held his arm up in the air, water dripping from the sleeve of his blue jumper, and shuddered with revulsion. The moss fell into the water and slid away downstream. He picked up his boat and climbed on to the wooden bridge and put on his sandals, rubbing his wrist against the cloth of his trousers. 'I don't like that,' he said out loud. From somewhere behind him he could hear voices, high up on the hillside, up there where the pines grew. He twisted his head and thought he saw pieces of another hut, painted white, fragmented by the branches of the trees. He began to run up the steep slope towards Hut 4.

He had to stop after a time; he was just too tired. He wasn't cold any more. His cheeks burned and the fringe of hair clung to his forehead. Everything was motionless about him, everything just like a painting he might do at school: all the leaves on all the trees exactly in their places, bits of green paper cut into ragged shapes and gummed against the sky. The hut was up there beyond that beech tree and if he climbed the slope he would be there, except that he must go by the path because the other way there might be nettles and nests of wild bees and perhaps even a snake. His father would never

21

bother with the path, or George, but then his father had big rubber gumboots that crushed the nettles underfoot and George was the tallest man in the world and nothing could harm him.

Slowly he continued along the path. His mother, he thought, would probably be missing him now or having a rest on the Victorian sofa in the living room, all her hair in little curls about her neck and one fat hand clutching her handkerchief. When she woke she would call his name and then reach for her cigarettes; they would be near but he wouldn't be. She had told him over and over to be nice to Joseph and to give him lots of kisses and not to tire him too much. Lots of kisses he told himself, watching his sandalled feet go along the path, curving round the hillside towards his father.

Then he remembered that Balfour had mentioned that there was another hut beyond the bushes, above the path. George had made it himself out of planks of wood, and inside there was a lavatory – not a proper one but a big can with a chemical inside that killed all the germs. Roland looked at the grass, pressed flat by the recent rain and thought of all the germs multiplying beneath the trees. Balfour had said that George had made all the huts in the forest, with the help of Mr MacFarley and Willie, the odd-job man from the village. Roland looked beyond the bushes and saw the square black hut with its door swinging open. He approached it from the side and searched with his hands on the rough wood for the heads of nails, but he couldn't feel any. Then he bent down and looked under the hut and saw that it was built against the hillside at the back and that the front was propped level with red bricks. The grass underneath had died; it was colourless like glass. Between the mortar of the bricks he could see a spider's web, the same shade as the dead grass. He put his head on a level with the ground and looked for the spider, but it wasn't there. Something moved within the hut.

22

He saw Kidney, frowning and ham pink, seated with his corduroy trousers in folds about his ankles.

'What are you doing?'

'I'm on the lavatory,' said Kidney. Earnestly he gazed past Roland at some point beyond the trees.

'You have got white legs.' Roland looked at Kidney's knees. In the gloom of the little hut they glowed. 'Funny,' he said, 'because you've got such a red face.' He stepped back and examined the hut again. 'You do look nice, Kidney. All those leaves round the door and you in your little house sitting there.'

Kidney shifted himself on the seat but said nothing.

'Have you got any toilet paper?' Roland asked him.

'Yes, thank you.'

'Are you sitting on the germs?'

Kidney wouldn't answer.

Roland kicked at the door with his foot and it swung inwards and back again.

'Go away,' Kidney said.

Obediently Roland ran away up the path to Hut 4 to find his father. He found him on his knees beside the wicker basket. With a nail file Joseph was turning a screw in a white plug.

'What's that for?' Roland squatted down beside him and watched the shiny screw come loose.

'My electric razor. I'm trying to mend it.'

'But you've got a beard.'

'I know.' He probed with the nail file at the veins of red wire, sucking a strand of beard between his full lips.

'William hasn't got a beard,' said Roland. William was his mother's friend, who missed his last bus home sometimes and was in the bathroom in the morning, standing before the gold mirror, scraping soap off his chin.

'Oh well,' said Joseph. 'I like to keep my neck tidy.'

'It's a super toilet,' said Roland. He lay on the floor and

23

spread his arms wide as if he were swimming.

'Lavatory, not toilet,' Joseph told him. 'Toilet's too damn refined.'

'They say toilet at school.' To add weight he added, 'Mummy says toilet.' He moved his legs up and down in the invisible sea. 'It's all black and leaves all round the door – and that bastard Kidney sitting on the can of germs.'

'Don't you like Kidney?' Joseph sat back on his heels and spat shreds of wire out of his mouth.

'Yes,' said Roland. He stopped swimming and looked round the hut. 'Don't expect there's anywhere to put your plug here.' He looked carefully at all the places where plugs might go if this were home.

For a moment his father was silent. Then he shrugged his shoulders and opened the lid of the basket and dropped the plug and nail file inside. 'How right you are,' he said, getting up from his knees and wiping dust from his trousers.

Kidney entered the hut and saw Joseph at the mirror, legs braced wide apart, combing his hair back behind his ears.

'Wash your hands,' Joseph said, putting the comb away. 'We're going over to George's hut for tea.' He avoided looking directly at Kidney. Roland had opened the wicker basket and was holding the useless plug in his hands. 'Put that down,' his father told him.

Blushing, Roland dropped the plug into the basket and fiddled with the strap of his brown sandal. He didn't like being shouted at in front of Kidney.

At the far end of the hut, at the sink, Kidney dried his hands carefully on the red towel which Joseph had placed on a hook above the draining board. The towel was one from the flat that Joseph lived in, that he lived in too. He used it in the mornings before going to college with Joseph. He used to go to college every day, but recently Joseph hadn't come into his room in the mornings and he had lain there in his bed listening to the sound of Joseph doing his exercises, the tea being made, the soft buzzing noise of the electric shaver as Joseph tidied his

24

neck and throat, the footsteps running downstairs, the slam of the door and the final sound of the car being started. Only then did he leave his bed and go to the window, staring along the street in the direction in which Joseph had gone, imagining he saw the vapour of the exhaust still rising in the empty road. Then he would wander from room to room, not knowing what to do, picking up the book of poems given him by Joseph, not reading them – he had never read them – just holding the thin book in his hands. Sometimes Dotty came out of the bedroom in a long nightgown and a face white as chalk, not looking at him at all, not seeing him, as if he didn't exist, looking only for the box of matches. He turned to face Joseph, nervously crumpling the towel in his rubbed dry hands.

'Do you want me to come?'

'Of course, you silly bastard.'

'I thought I might stay here and read a book. I don't feel very hungry.' Kidney looked down at the floor, lost in a vision of being alone while they had tea, sitting with a book, a good book, and reading all the words, alone in the empty hut.

Abruptly Joseph said, 'Oh, stay if you want to', and strode out. Roland struggled to his feet and ran after him. Kidney heard him call 'Wait for me'. Then Joseph's head appeared at the window. 'Come on, Kidney,' he said gently. 'Come and have some tea with us.' Almost tenderly he added, 'We want you to come.'

Smiling, Kidney lumbered out of the hut.

2

After a supper of sausages, followed by cups of coffee, Roland
had been put to bed in the long barn at the back of the hut. He
had protested at being couched out there, alone in the field.
Privately Dotty had agreed with him, thinking he was too little
and too spoiled to rest easy away from the main hut. She had
kept her opinion to herself, fearing Joseph might remember
why it was the child couldn't sleep with him, deciding at the
recollection that it was unjust, and that she, not his lovely boy,
must sleep in the barn with only a strip of brown carpet edged
with mud between her and the restless Kidney. Guiltily she
watched Roland carried from the hut in his father's arms.

'Look up there,' Joseph entreated, standing in the damp
grass under the black sky, wanting Roland to observe the
stars. But Roland wouldn't raise his head. In the darkness a
bird flew from a swaying tree. Roland made sounds of misery.
Once in bed, laid down in the puffy darkness, Joseph told him
to be a good boy and go to sleep.

'Tomorrow,' he said, stroking the child's head, 'I'm going
to take you up the mountain. Just you and me. We'll be
explorers. We'll go very early,' he continued, soothing himself
as much as the child, 'and we'll see the tower and we'll look
down and see the countryside spread out just like a map.'

'I don't like being here alone,' whispered Roland in despair.

Joseph tucked the rough blankets more firmly round the
boy. 'You won't be alone. Kidney is going to sleep in the other
bed. We're all going to bed shortly.' His voice receded toward
the door. 'Now go to sleep, Roland, and no more nonsense.

I'm only next door. You're not alone ... Good night, boy.' To which Roland wouldn't reply, leaving his father no alternative but to shut the door and stumble back over the grass to the paraffin-lit hut.

Roland, in bed, wiped at his face with the sheet and thought how cross his mother would be when he told her how frightened he had been at night. Soundlessly his lips shaped the words betraying his father, and he saw her face looming before him, eyes widening at the terrible story, her teeth set like pegs between her lips. 'All alone, my little boy, left all alone.' He looked up at the square of window above his head, trying to see the stars, but the glass was too thick and he didn't dare kneel upright in the bed. He remembered something his teacher had told him about stars, how they weren't really there, only the light coming down every night for ever. Maybe his mother would buy him a train set to make up for him being so unhappy out there in the wood.

In the hut Joseph was trying to justify his treatment of his son. 'You were an only child,' he told the placid George. 'Do you feel you were deprived or lonely as a boy?'

'No,' said George.

Balfour, dabbing his eyes with a square of handkerchief, saw that Joseph was regarding him attentively. 'Hay fever,' he apologised and blew his nose violently.

Dotty rose and went to the end of the hut. She pulled the wicker basket out from under the settee and rummaged inside. Crouched sideways on her haunches, chin down, she looked like an athlete landing after a pole vault.

'What are you doing?' Joseph asked.

'Getting the Chablis.'

'What on earth for?'

'Because I feel like a drink.' She stood up and walked to the table, not putting down the wine, face sullen in the yellow light. 'I did buy it with my own money. Have you a bottle opener, George?'

Balfour went into the kitchen, taking with him the paraffin

27

lamp, leaving the others in near-darkness, finding the corkscrew hanging from a nail on the wall. He thought, not for the first time, surveying the pan scrubbers and ladles, the weighing scales, the cake trays, the jars of herbs in a row on the shelf, that there were more things in this hut than in most normal houses. He brought the corkscrew and the light back into the room.

'Here we are,' he said, giving Dotty the corkscrew and going back for the glasses. Dotty withdrew the cork herself.

'Must be fair,' she said, pouring the colourless liquid into the tumblers.

'Why only four glasses?' asked Joseph in triumph, anxious to put her in the wrong. He turned to look at the corner of the hut where Kidney was sitting, face completely in shadow, only his legs and feet illuminated.

Balfour hurried to fetch another glass from the kitchen.

When they were all drinking, Joseph leaned forward in his chair and looking directly at Balfour asked, 'What do you do?'

'I'm in a factory.' Tongue thick with alarm, Balfour moistened his worker lips. 'That is, I'm a tool-fitter.' He drank quickly, disliking the taste, hearing Joseph say, 'A tool-fitter. How very obscene, but fascinating, I'm sure. A man who works with his hands.'

'Not with his hands,' said George. 'With machines.'

Gratefully Balfour echoed, 'That's right. I work with machines.'

'It's not very fascinating either,' added George, swilling his wine round in the thick tumbler. 'He's been wanting to escape for years. My father says, – his shoulders slumped somewhat, as some part of him always did at mention of Mr MacFarley – 'that Balfour is needed for better things than machines.'

Oh God, blasphemed the inward Balfour, hating to be reminded of the better things. He drank his wine, not noticing the taste as much.

'What things do you feel you are needed for?' asked Joseph.

'I-I don't feel that I'm needed at all,' said Balfour. 'It's Mr

MacFarley that seems to think that. I don't think about it.'

'Ah come now, tell me,' Joseph persisted. 'Tell me the truth. What do you do with your life apart from your machines?'

'I w-work with young people,' said Balfour. Then, in a rush, feeling liberated by the wine and compelled to answer, he added: 'We have a c-club and we take lads into the country and we bring them here.' Giving credit where credit was due, he continued: 'Mr and Mrs MacFarley and George let us have the huts and we let them climb the mountain and we try to help them appreciate the c-countryside.'

'It sounds marvellous,' said Joseph, 'and very unselfish. Now me, I'm afraid – I'd find it difficult to devote my time to young people in that way for so little return.'

Dotty banged her glass down contemptuously on the table.

Balfour wanted to ask Joseph what he was doing with Kidney if it wasn't to help him, but he didn't know exactly what Kidney's problems were and he couldn't guess the kind of returns Joseph meant. Instead he said, gulping his Chablis: 'But there's enormous returns. It's very r-rewarding, believe me. I could tell you a lot of things about that. Very r-rewarding.' He was aware that his speech was becoming unsteady. Shaking his head, he affirmed: 'Very rewarding. If you c-could see the kind of homes I go into in the course of my d-duties you'd know what I mean. You see, I go to some houses to f-find out why some kid hasn't been to the club and there's a bloody big tenement block of flats with a stone courtyard like a kind of barrack square and I ...'

'I know exactly what you mean,' interrupted Joseph with enthusiasm. 'Terrible architecture, no sense of community life, no feeling of life at all. How can people grow and flourish with such ugliness all around them? How can their lives possibly have meaning?'

'Light is needed,' said George, 'and space and a better use of concrete. Ideally they should build their own dwellings to their own needs.'

Jesus, thought Balfour, hanging his head in defeat.

Joseph continued, 'You see, in proper planning they'd know that people need to be in a community. They'd know that ugly surroundings imprison a man and that beauty liberates him. They'd use colours and play areas and they'd leave the trees standing.'

'The trees should be left,' said Balfour. 'I agree they should leave the trees. B-but half the bloody kids in the flats would pull them out by the roots. And they did try a playground bit in the new flats and a square of green, down in Windsor Street, and every morning you couldn't see the grass for the f-french letters.'

Joseph laughed, leaning his head back and bringing his hands down hard on his knees to express his approval.

'It's more than grass that's needed,' Balfour said. 'It's not a question of needing to flourish. It's more just l-living that's wanted. There's this woman, Mrs Conran, with a lad called Billy – she's got a grown daughter with two kids of her own in the same two-roomed flat and Billy suddenly doesn't turn up at the club or school for that matter. So I go to see her and I say, putting my foot in the door, "Hallo, Mrs Conran," – they love that – "How's your Billy? Wondered why he hasn't been to the club like." And she says, "Our Billy's sick, Mr Whatsit." And I say, "Can I come in and have a word with him, Mrs Conran?" And she says, "He's sick like, Mr Whatsit." Anyway I get into the place and in a cot in the room is Mrs Conran's daughter's two kids, both under three, sucking milk from a Tizer bottle. Billy Conran's lying on a blanket on the floor with his face turned to the wall, and a bloody big growth just like a mushroom growing on the plaster above his head, and I say, "Not so good, eh, Billy lad? Wondered why you didn't come to the club like." And Billy's not saying a word because he can't put two words together anyway, and Mrs Conran says, "It's like he don't want to face the world, Mr Whatsit." Can you beat that?' Balfour let the words keep coming. 'And while I'm trying to figure that one out, in comes Mrs Conran's daughter from the kitchen with a fella and Ma

Conran says, 'Mr Whatsit's here, Lil', and Lil goes back into the kitchen with her drawers in her hand and the bloke goes out of the door and Billy just lies there ...'

'There've been worse things,' George said, 'much worse things. Systematic killing.'

'Oh Christ,' groaned Balfour irritably. 'Don't start that again.' He belched loudly.

'I've not seen him like this before,' said George.

Balfour raised his head in defiance, but it was suddenly too heavy for his neck and he leaned over his knees, thinking about some baby in a bath that he had wanted to drown. He had wanted to flush the baby down the plug hole, fat legs kicking ... going bell-tinkle ... whose baby ...? 'Who's fatty?' he asked Joseph suddenly looking up.

'Who is fatty?' articulated Joseph smiling. 'No idea, old chap.'

The rocking chair thudded forward as George vacated it. 'I think he'd better go to bed ... I think my father would like him to go to bed.'

'Are you receiving telepathic information or something? Is that it?' Joseph wagged his finger at George, not sure if his voice was sufficiently jocular. He didn't want to upset George. Changing the subject he asked, as if interested, which he wasn't, 'Is his name really Balfour, George? I mean, is it Balfour something, or something Balfour?'

Hearing his name, the tool-fitter swung his head from side to side.

'The declaration of the Jewish state,' said George at the doorway, propping it open with his back, watching the sway of his scarf ends in the night air.

'He's off again,' moaned Balfour.

'His name is Edgar Balfour,' said George. 'I think he ought to go to bed. He's been ill for a long time.'

'Ill?' Dotty regarded the flushed Balfour. 'What's wrong with him?'

'Just ill.'

Balfour tried to concentrate. Joseph was saying something,

31

something about the people due to arrive tomorrow. He must attend. There might, who knows, be a message.

'She's a blonde,' said Joseph, 'and he's in some sort of business. He used to be in the Army. Had his buttock shot off in Italy.'

George said without reproach, listening to an owl hoot somewhere behind the long barn, 'You didn't say there was a woman coming.'

'Didn't I? Oh well, they're married, George. It's not too bad.'

Dear God, thought Balfour, practically sobered with shock. Not two men but a man and wife – a woman with yellow hair and a man with a mutilated arse, in his hut, sleeping in the same room as himself. He removed his hands from his face and gazed at Joseph hopelessly.

'Bed.' Joseph yawned, gripping the edges of his chair to lever his body upright. 'Tomorrow, Mr Whatsit, we really must have a long talk about your social work, old chap.'

I must try to be cheerful and off-hand, thought Dotty, her fingers still clasping her empty glass. Either that or I must pretend to be asleep.

Order and growth, thought George, staring out into the dark field, thinking of his remembrance trees, his thousand memorials, each one named in memory of a Jew who had never reached the Promised Land.

They moved in several directions to bed. Kidney was dispatched to the barn, taken to the door by lamplight and thrust inside. 'Don't wake Roland,' hissed Joseph fiercely, shutting him away for the night.

'Goodnight – goodnight,' they told each other, close now that they were about to separate.

George lit a candle for Dotty and Joseph because he needed the lamp to guide the unsteady Balfour down the slope and across the stream to Hut 2. 'You can have carpets you can afford at Cyril Lord,' sang the stumbling Balfour in the darkness.

3

Willie came across the fields from Calfin shortly after seven o'clock the following morning. He took his time, not on account of his years but because there was no need to hurry and because, since his retirement from the mines, he had begun to suffer increasingly from shortness of breath. While the wife still slept he had struggled into his clothes and gone down the narrow stairs into the kitchen to make himself a cup of tea. He hadn't bothered to eat. He found he had three Woodbines left from the night before, and the visitors over at Nant MacFarley might possibly tip him for cleaning out the toilet. He would buy some bacon at the corner shop for breakfast on his way back from the Glen. He let himself out quietly, treading gently down the path so as not to disturb the wife. She would probably want to know why he was going and where and what for, and he didn't want to discuss it. He had married late, after the death of his mother, and mostly he confused the two women in his mind.

At the crossroads his footsteps faltered as if, by rights, by habit, his boots should go left towards the pit. He spat frequently into the grass as he went, walking with legs well-bent at the knee, eyes darting from side to side under the colourless brim of his cap, seeing little pictures – a brown bottle, unbroken, upright in a patch of thistle, a line of sheep two meadows distant, pouring like grey milk through a gap in the hedge, the mountain humped behind a scroll of mist. His lips moved as he climbed, telling himself it was a good morning, over and over like a prayer, letting his body go with the flow of the hill so as to conserve his energy.

The cows in the top field were still lying down across the daisies. He didn't see the daisies, but he saw the cows out of the corner of one pale blue eye: seven cows in a lump under an elm tree.

He rested a moment astride the stile above the Big House. Removing one of the three saved Woodbines out of his jacket pocket, he rolled it between his fingers to coax it back into plumpness.

He liked to keep an eye on the Glen when the MacFarleys were away. He didn't consider Master George man enough to be responsible, not being a married man, and there were so many jobs likely to be overlooked. In his working days he had come to lend a hand on a Sunday after chapel, and every day on his paid week's absence from the mines, even when he was off sick, if he could manage to get away without the wife nagging him too much and going on about him being dishonest to the company. Since his retirement he came and went as he chose. Some people had their clubs or their bingo or their dart matches: he had his Glen.

Spitting shreds of tobacco from his flat lips he shambled down the slope, skirting the Big House and George's bedroom, not wanting to be greeted until he had introduced himself to the visitors in Hut 4, going down into the valley with lips still moving and chest still heaving.

George, though not the first to wake, was the first to leave his bed some few minutes after Willie had passed the wall of his room. He dressed and folded his sleeping bag neatly before going through to the kitchen of the Big House. There he washed his hands and face. He was happy because Joseph was in the Glen and there would be things to talk about. George had had a solitary childhood, albeit in a boarding school, and a solitary manhood, though he wasn't conscious of any deprivation. He liked order and he liked company of a sort, Joseph's sort. Joseph on occasions had discussed Art with him in a way that he found suitable and in conformity with his own sense of order. If he had known that Joseph was to all men all things and to his own self nothing, it wouldn't have spoiled his pleasure or diminished his admiration.

Balfour had woken shivering an hour or so earlier, minus his boots but otherwise fully clothed, with parched mouth and gelatine eyelids. He burrowed into his sleeping bag, handsewn by George, thought once about the one-arsed brigadier due to arrive that day, and drifted again into sleep.

Joseph and Dotty were lying side by side in the single bed in Hut 4. Their two faces were cold under the beamed roof. On the chest of drawers Joseph had stood his after-shave lotion, a bottle of green scented water with a spray given to him by his ex-wife at Christmas. It looked like a floral arrangement with a single bud, propped against the brown wall of the cabin.

Outside the hut trod Willie, spitting his phlegm into the undergrowth, noting that the washing line had gone from its place slung between the blackthorn thicket and the elder bush. He scratched his neck under the band of his cap and saw the rope hanging from the high elm at the boundary of the field. However did it get up there, he asked himself out loud, looking up into the sky? Puzzled, he shook his head and went down the path.

Only Kidney had made use of the shed in the bushes. In the night Dotty had woken fretfully and fumbled awkwardly under the truckle bed for the chamber pot placed there by Mrs MacFarley. As if triggered to wake at just such a moment, Joseph had risen invisibly in the blacker-than-black night and said 'Out, out' and folded like a wing to the mattress again. Obediently Dotty had gone and squatted under the dark sky, pissing reproachfully into the damp grass. Moth-pale in her voluminous nightgown, she had crouched with splayed knees, thinking that no doubt Roland and daft Kidney would be permitted the solace of a chamber pot, but not she, being female. Waddling experimentally forward, she had felt like some duck threading its way through platters of water lilies in a pond. She stood, trying to list all the animal names of the stars that swam about day and night above the earth: the winged horse, the dolphin, the eagle, the horned goat, the scorpion, the serpent, the bull, the little bear. Little bear gone away, she had told herself fancifully, climbing back into bed beside the superior Joseph, thinking of the dreams he must be dreaming.

Willie first of all took off his coat and hung it on the inner door of the lavatory. Then, bending low, as if to perform a Russian dance movement, he embraced the pan with his two short arms and lifted it from the cement hole in the base of the shed. He carried it up the slope past Hut 4 to a place behind the long barn. Grunting, he put his burden down on the wet patch of ground and rested a moment with hands to his side before going to fetch his spade from beneath the uprights of Hut 4. He began to dig a deep hole.

Roland opened his eyes in the middle of a dream about the baby who belonged to the people next door. He saw the baby's face on the pillow beside him, larger than it should be and crowned with hair, but with the same crumpled mouth and the same skin, shiny as the white candle his mother had in the brass holder in the living room. He blinked his eyes, and then saw that it was only Kidney's face after all lying there above the sheet. He sat up in bed and looked about him at the barn. It was a bit like a ship, he thought, with all those wooden walls and the planks joined together by nails big as sixpences. There was a clothing rack hanging just beneath the arch of the roof, tethered to the wall of the hut by a rope wound in a figure of eight about an iron hook. He trod along the side of the blanketed bed, careful not to step on the baby-faced Kidney, and climbed over the black-painted bars to the floor. He took his trousers and his jumper in his arms and kicking his sandals before him opened the barn door and stepped down into the grass.

The place had changed completely from what he remembered. For one thing, there was a smell of something, and there were trees everywhere – no longer grey, but all sorts of colours. Among the bushes near the barn there were pieces of flowers, blue and white, and just by the front step of the hut in which his father was sleeping a marigold grew in the grass, a wasp flying about its head. Bravely he approached the hut door from the opposite side, leaning across the wooden step, fumbling with the knob, keeping his eyes fixed on the spiralling wasp. Dismayed, he dropped his clothes and retreated further away from the marigold, never letting the insect out of his sight. He could hear someone digging behind the barn, but he didn't care to go that far, without his sandals. Spinning round and round in the field, he shouted 'Daddy, Daddy'. In the middle of his pirouette he saw the swing his father had made in the elm tree and righting himself he ran to the loop hanging above the grass.

Facing away from the barn and hut, he sat on the horizontal bar, which was wide enough for him alone, and pushed with his muddy feet at the bumpy ground, rocking forward into the field. After a time he rose above the level of the tangled hedgerow and saw the mountain in the distance. Mouth open, he slid backwards through the leafy field and wriggling his body from side to side slowed the swing. At a point nearest the ground he jumped clear and rolled down the wet slope. Forgetting the wasp, forgetting his fear of snakes and worms, he ran round the back of the hut and squatting on his haunches banged with his hand on the small window behind which he knew his father lay. 'The mountain,' he shouted, pushing his nose to the pane of glass, seeing Dotty with her face turned towards him and her eyes closed but no sign of

Joseph. Fist clenched, he continued to beat at the window, heart pounding with the vision of the mountain he had seen.

Joseph woke from a dream. He sat up and saw his son outside the window. 'Hallo, boy,' he mouthed, leaping from the bed clad only in a string vest. He was furious with himself for letting Roland see Dotty and him in the same bed. He picked up his clothes hastily and ran to unlock the front door, stubbing his toe as he did so. He kissed the boy with a great show of cheerfulness, making a lot of incidental noises, hissing with feigned hurt and holding his foot in the air, saying 'Ooooh' with pursed lips, spitting with laughter as Roland jumped in his arms.

Roland had never, to Joseph's knowledge, caught him in bed with a woman. Joseph didn't believe anyway that a child of eight – or was it seven? – equated bed with sex. Still, he was upset as he wrestled with the child. Hastily he dressed, hopping in the grass with Roland clinging to his ankle. Somebody coughed beyond the hut. Taking Roland by the hand, Joseph went to investigate.

Behind the barn he saw the old fellow who worked for the MacFarleys – the odd-job man, Bertie or Tommy or someone.

Touching his cap, Willie said, 'And how are you, Mr Joseph?'

'Fine, fine. Must't complain. Digging, I see.'

'Just emptying the toilet for you, Mr Joseph. Start clean, as it were. Mr MacFarley likes me to keep an eye on things.'

'We've not actually gone into production yet,' said Joseph. He wondered how much the old chap would expect to be tipped. 'Go and get your clothes on, Roland,' he ordered.

'Got your hands full,' said Willie, leaning on his spade, taking in Mr Joseph's trousers and jacket. Best London style, he thought: bit of a dandy – and a woman back there in the hut very possibly, if he ran true to previous years.

Sensing criticism, Joseph said, 'He's no trouble, we get on very well. Nodding to Willie, he went into the hut, and after a moment Willie followed him.

When Dotty got up she found Joseph in the kitchen making breakfast. Roland was at the table, eating fried bread and bacon. Thankfully she saw the old man drinking tea. Joseph was always better in the morning if there was someone else around, someone he wasn't on intimate terms with. It meant he wouldn't start telling her she was a lazy bitch, which she suspected she was.

'This is Dotty,' Joseph said, coming forward to pat her shoulder.

'Good morning,' said Willie, not looking at her long face nor her long hair. 'Come up from London, have you?' he asked, stamping his feet and wheezing.

'Yes, from London,' Dotty told him. She sat down beside Roland at the table, looking at his half-consumed fried bread and bacon longingly. She was always hungry and she always felt guilty at being hungry – not at home with her parents, or in a café, but anywhere where Joseph was. He made her feel greedy or something. She asked him for a cup of tea, keeping her face turned away from him, because there hadn't been a mirror in the cubicle and she didn't know whether her make-up was grimy from the night before. Her hair, she knew, was untidy, but she wasn't sure where her comb might be and even if she had known Joseph would be irritable if she did her hair in the kitchen and more irritable if she left the room just as she had entered. He could run in and out like a restless sheepdog and trim his beard over the bacon and eggs, but then he was male and therefore not disgusting. She asked Roland if he had slept well.

'Yes,' the child answered flatly, crunching fried bread in his mouth.

'He's been running about the fields in his pyjamas since dawn,' said Joseph. He added meaningfully: 'Couldn't get in at the door, so he banged on the window.'

'It wasn't dawn, it was day, and I didn't run around. Actually, I went on the swing,' said Roland.

'My God,' cried Joseph, face animated above the spitting

fat. 'It was the swing – that was it.'

'Oh aye,' Willie said. 'I saw you took down Mrs MacFarley's washing line.'

'I dreamt about Kidney playing with a rope – not here, back at the flat,' said Joseph. 'He was sitting on the floor, the studio floor, coiling this rope round and round his waist. He had a funny expression, Dotty, really very strange.' Needing her interest, for the toilet-cleansing Welshman couldn't possibly understand the special significance of such a dream, Joseph gave his full attention to the famished Dotty. 'There was a record on the gramophone – I can't remember what record – and there was someone else there ...' Joseph frowned, wrinkling his forehead, holding the pan of bacon away from the stove.

'Nathan,' said Dotty. She resented his everlasting nights of symbolic imagery. She herself dreamed mostly that she was being betrayed or tortured or conned by Joseph. She could never remember the whole of her dreams, and if she was asked she made something up. Still when Joseph spoke so directly to her, treating her as if she were real to him, she was forced to respond. Apart from that, she loved him and she didn't want to hurt him.

'Of course, Nathan.' Delighted, Joseph smiled at her. Nathan was the cat.

'I dreamed the baby next door was in my bed,' Roland said.

'The baby next door was in your bed,' repeated Joseph fondly, still thinking of the rope about the thick waist of Kidney.

'But when I woke up it was only Kidney,' said Roland.

'Only Kidney,' said Joseph. 'Only Kidney! In your bed? Surely not?'

The child didn't reply, absorbed in thoughts of the baby next door. Sometimes when the baby's parents went out – to a party or something – they left it with his mother and it slept in a cot in his room. In the mornings Roland would wake and see it standing in a long nightie at the end of the cot, peering through the bars at him. It had a pinkish face with no eyebrows and no teeth either and just a few shreds of hair, the colour of marmalade, on its plump head. If he went towards the cot the baby lifted up its arms and tried to pull itself up out of the bed. His mother had warned him never to lift the baby out on his own, but he often did, until one morning the baby slipped backwards into the cot and fell with its head against the bars. His mother came running then and lifted the baby up, and after a while she let Roland cuddle it. He was sad and excited at having hurt it, and he put his face down into the fold of its neck, where it smelt like an apple, and he cried too.

'Roland, I'm talking to you. Was Kidney in your bed?'

'Yes, he was.'

'What the hell did he get into Roland's bed for?' asked Joseph helplessly, looking at Dotty with raised eyebrows.

'Probably couldn't see in the dark,' she said reasonably.

'But he shouldn't have.'

'Why not?' asked Roland, leaving the table and going to the door of the hut. He peered over at the marigold and was relieved to see that the wasp had gone.

'Well, he shouldn't have.' At a loss, his father put back his frying pan on the gas and continued his cooking.

'I didn't mind.' Roland came back to the table and leaned against Dotty. 'Did you mind Daddy being in your bed?'

'No,' Dotty said, stirring her tea and wanting her comb.

Willie spent most of the morning hanging about the barn and Hut 4, anxious not to miss anything and with plenty to think about. He filled the lavatory pan with an equal amount of chemical and water and replaced it on its base in the shed among the bushes. Nobody appeared to take advantage of his gesture. He refilled the crater he had made, burying Kidney's waste matter, and burned some rubbish left by Balfour several weeks ago.

The girl in the nightgown wandered about the field for some time before getting dressed, looking at the flowers in the

41

hedgerows and lighting a lot of cigarettes she rolled herself. She dropped matches and stub ends all over the place. She went and sat on the swing too, gliding over the grass with her nightgown billowing out behind her and her two thin yellow feet pointing at the sky. Mr George, Willie thought, would be grim-faced about all those fag-ends littering the place. He was a tidy sort like his father, though not half the man his father was. In the middle of the morning Mr Joseph went into the barn. There was a lot of shouting, and after a while a boy came out into the sunshine with a mop of hair and a face pretty as a girl, prettier than most. Mr Joseph said it was too late for breakfast now, nearly lunchtime in fact. He told the lad he was too fat anyway, which was about the size of it – a big soft lump of a lad, just standing there shuffling his feet and blushing and saying he was sorry. After a bit more talk, too low-pitched for Willie to catch, the lad began taking off his shirt and his vest and there was a pair of breasts good enough for a woman, if you didn't like them too big. White little swellings turning pinkish, for all the world like the buds on the Norway maple down in the Glen, and not a sign of hair on the padded chest nor beneath the armpits. This last fact Willie established when Joseph had hoisted the youth on to the branch of the tree, letting him dangle by his arms above the slope. He was supposed to raise his legs, but he just hung there with his face filling with blood.

4

At mid-day when Joseph was checking the food stores he was depressed to realise that the supply he had brought to last three or four days was barely going to feed them for today. It was Dotty eating half the bacon at one go. Where had the grapefruit gone and the three boxes of cheese segments? Righteously indignant, he thundered her name from the doorway, agitating Willie who was taking his ease at the back of the barn, sitting in the long grass with his cigarette alight and his cap over his eyes.

'What's up now?' Willie asked himself out loud.

Again the girl's name was called, louder this time.

Grinning because it wasn't he Mr Joseph was after, Willie relaxed and drew on his Woodbine.

After a while, for she had been down at the stream with Roland when the summons came, Dotty appeared at the door of the hut, a little out of breath from her climb up the slope. She had been dreaming all the time she ran up the path that above in the holiday hut love waited. Love had suddenly seized Joseph by the throat and dragged him to the edge of the forest to call her name. Either that or he had found her lost comb which she hadn't washed for weeks or the soiled underwear she had stuffed into the wicker basket under the settee.

She said 'Yes?', looking at his humourless face as he put

43

down knives and forks on the dinner table.

'Where's the cheese and where's the grapefruit juice?'

'The grapefruit juice?'

'The grapefruit juice.'

He was emptying salt from a packet into an egg cup. All the work there would be when they left, she thought – putting butter in glass bowls and Roland's tomato sauce into a gravy jug. Such a fuss. Relieved that it wasn't her comb or the state of her bra, she said, 'If you mean the grapefruit juice we got on the Finchley Road, it's in the fridge at the flat.'

'At the flat?'

'You said it was too big to go in the grocery box, so we didn't bring it. And the cheese is in the tin on the shelf.'

'Do you realise we have only enough food for today?'

It didn't surprise her at all. He'd brought rice and raisins but no potatoes or tins of Heinz beans or anything they could live on.

'It means,' said Joseph, bitterly, 'that I'll have to shop again tomorrow. I've already spent a bomb.'

Dotty sat down at the table.

'You're slouching,' he said. 'Here, cut up some onions. I'm making a rice thing for lunch.'

'Roland won't eat it,' she said.

Joseph didn't reply. She chopped gamely at the onions he placed in front of her.

'Do you think,' he asked, 'that I ought to say something to Kidney? About his being in Roland's bed?'

'I don't know,' said Dotty. 'What *could* you say?'

'I could mention the bed's not big enough for two. He might say something – give some explanation.'

'I doubt it,' Dotty said. 'Are you worried about sex or something?'

'Don't be ridiculous,' snapped Joseph. But he was worried. When he had suggested having Kidney to live with him, the doctor at the clinic Kidney attended had asked him if there were any women living in the house. Joseph hadn't mentioned

44

Dotty because he hadn't thought of her as being a permanent fixture.

'He was probably just cold,' said Dotty. 'I'd forget about it. If he was really bonkers – I mean, dangerous – he'd be in a home.' She stood up and turned the gas lower under the pan of bubbling rice. It still mystified her how Joseph had managed to get permission to take care of Kidney.

'He has been in a home,' said Joseph. 'Several in fact. Leave that rice alone.'

She did as she was told. The rice was almost done and with any luck it might stick to the bottom of the pan. She went and sat on the settee at the end of the hut, feeling with the heels of her feet for the wicker basket, watching Joseph scrape the cut onions and the paprikas into the frying pan. When he turned his back to place the vegetables on the stove she leant forward and put her fingers under the lid of the basket, trying to locate her bra. But she couldn't.

'Go and call Roland,' bade Joseph, turning the contents of the pan with a knife. 'And see if Kidney is at the back of the barn with Tommy.'

'Willie,' corrected Dotty, going out into the field.

Joseph shook the pan about briskly, causing mushroom buds to fall among the paprikas and the pale rings of onion. He thought, Degas or Delacroix or someone like that had made a work of art once out of an omelette. What a pity Kidney had given up painting. Not that the results were all that stimulating – dull little fields with puffy clouds – and he himself had to spend such hours clearing the mess up afterwards, the paint splashed on the wall and the smears of water on the table. It was a pity, but some time soon, very soon, he was going to have to turn Kidney over to someone else. It would mean he might have to go into a home again. But somehow, he'd lost interest. He could always visit the youth. 'Lunch,' he shouted, putting his head out of the window, seeing Dotty and Kidney on the path. 'Did you call Roland?'

45

'Yes,' she said.

When he came in, Roland ate the rice without complaint. 'What's that tree called?' he asked his father. 'The one beside the barn?'

As usual, he received no reply, for Joseph was listening to the sounds made by Willie hovering outside the hut.

'He's waiting for his bloody tip,' Joseph told Dotty, none too quietly, adding loudly for the benefit of the Welshman without, 'Like a cup of Nescafé?'

Willie didn't really want the drink. To tell the truth he was beginning to feel a bit peckish and regretful he hadn't gone home for some breakfast, but he did want to be amongst them – the woman and Mr Joseph and the plump young lad. What the devil was the lad doing along with Mr Joseph? 'Come up from London too?' he asked Kidney, removing his cap now he was indoors, wondering where to sit himself.

'Yes, from London too,' said Mr Joseph. Not a peep out of the lad himself, sitting there at the table with his cheeks like apples and his eyes shining. 'Sit down, Bill,' Mr Joseph told him, and there being no chair vacant he had to go to the end of the hut to the settee. He hadn't been called Bill since he was a boy and he sat very stiffly on the chintz settee with his shirt very full in the front, giving him a breast like a pigeon, and his red hair pressed flat to his head after being under his cap for so many hours. The girl looked as if she hadn't had a decent meal for God knows how long, spooning the food into her mouth, sitting with rounded shoulders. Mr Joseph had noted her shoulders. He was sitting very straight himself, in the manner of Mr MacFarley.

'Not at work today then, Bill?'

'Oh God no, Mr Joseph. I've been retired these six years. Seven more like.'

'Retired? Really.' Fixing his attention on Willie and off the hungry Dotty, Joseph made an attempt at conversation. 'Must find a lot of changes, being retired, Bill. Time hang heavy on your hands, does it?'

46

Dotty, hearing the mimicry of Willie's accent, scowled.

'Oh God no, I'm kept pretty busy here, you know. Always something to do, there is. Mr MacFarley's always got improvements in hand.' He wasn't sure that Mr Joseph was listening. At all events he was looking out at the field beyond the open door, leaning well back in his chair.

'Plenty to do,' said Willie, wondering when the girl would roll another cigarette and whether he would be offered one.

'I haven't seen old George this morning,' said Joseph.

'I have,' Roland said. 'He came down to the stream when I was playing with my boat. He told me not to fall in the water.'

'That's right,' Willie told him. 'Can't have you falling in the water.'

'He asked if you were up here,' said Roland. 'I said you were. I said you were digging a hole.'

'Oh, aye.' Mr George, Willie reflected, was no fool. Not the man his father was, but fairly shrewd. He'd be up here soon to ask why he was doing the toilet when it had been done only a day or so earlier. He'd best be getting off home soon.

'How do you get on with George?' asked Joseph suddenly, abandoning his food, laying down his fork and pushing the plate away.

'Well, now.' Willie dropped his cap to the floor. 'I can't say that I divine Mr George. I can't say that I do.'

'Very apt,' Joseph said, seeing in his mind the pigmy Welshman standing before the giant George, holding a divining rod towards the dark and elongated head.

'You see, it's like this, Mr Joseph. He was always a trifle odd, but he wasn't half so odd till he'd been to Israel –'

'To Israel?' said Joseph, startled.

'When he came back from Israel,' Willie said, 'he was a changed being and that's the truth. Even Mr MacFarley remarked on the change in him. Like as if he was mesmerised.'

'What's Israel?' Roland wanted to know, eating an orange on the floor.

'Where the Jews live,' his father told him. 'Get up and sit at

47

the table. No one said you could eat on the floor.'

The child stayed where he was, juice running from his lips.

'What's the red tree by the barn please, Willie?'

'The juniper tree, you mean – the one with the dark berries?'

'I didn't see any berries,' said Roland.

'Don't go eating any berries, my lad. You'll get belly-ache.'

'I think I'd better have one of my pills.' Kidney said, apparently to Willie. 'I should have one three times a day.'

Joseph said, 'I've decided to cut them out for a time. See what a bit of fresh air and exercise will do.' He began to put coffee powder into mugs of assorted colours.

'What's been wrong with Balfour?' asked Dotty. 'George said last night he'd been ill for a long time.' Dotty had been thinking about Balfour most of the morning.

Willie saw that she had already rolled one cigarette and was in the process of rolling another. In anticipation he said, 'Something wrong with his blood, I think, Mrs Dotty. I don't rightly know what. Thank you, I will.' He took the thin wafer she proferred him. 'He went away to Italy for a holiday some years back and picked up a germ. Kept him off work for quite a time. You see, it's like this. He gets sick suddenly – very high temperatures and the shivers, like as if he was turned to ice. All he can do is hide away and sleep it off.'

'How awkward,' remarked Joseph. He had little patience with sickness. How the hell, he wondered, had someone like Balfour afforded to go abroad. Not to mention George trotting round Israel. He bent and wiped at Roland's sticky mouth with the tea towel. If he wasn't so encumbered with responsibilities he might manage somewhere more exotic himself, though it would probably be the same wherever he went.

'Is Balfour ill now?' asked Dotty. But Willie was lighting his cigarette for the third time and pretended not to hear. He was a little tired of being the focal point of attention and he didn't much care for Balfour, hardly crediting why the MacFarleys had taken up with him in the first place.

'I think I ought to have a pill,' said Kidney loudly. 'I may get a bad headache otherwise.'

'Nonsense.' Brusquely Joseph placed a mug of coffee before him. 'Tell me, Bill, don't you find there's a sight too much pill-taking? Too many drugs and soporifics used today ... in comparison with when you were a boy? ... Don't you agree? ... Don't expect you saw the doctor much?'

'No ... no ...' Dismissing such pampering, Willie blew on his drink to cool it, looking down at his cigarette with disgust. The bloody thing was out again.

Pushing back his chair, Joseph said briskly, 'Right. Everybody out. Lionel will be arriving soon. I don't care what you do but leave me to tidy up.' Energetically he piled plates and stacked mugs. Willie, unable to ask for his tip, went out feeling cheated.

'Aren't you ever going to come and play with me and my boat?' said Roland.

'Later, boy, later. Go on, move.' Joseph pushed both the child and Dotty towards the door. Kidney stood up.

'Just a moment, Kidney,' said Joseph. 'Something I want to ask you.'

Kidney sat down again.

'I did tell you last night not to disturb Roland,' began Joseph. 'I did say to be quiet.'

Kidney stared at him.

'I did say that, didn't I?'

'Yes,' said Kidney.

'Well?'

'I didn't disturb him, Joseph.'

'You got into his bed.'

'Yes, Joseph.'

'Well?'

'I didn't disturb him, Joseph.'

'But why did you get into his bed?' Joseph took away the plates and dumped them in the sink.

The boy looked at him as if to speak. Instead he turned his eyes towards the doorway and studied the field.

Trying to reach him another way Joseph seated himself at the table. 'Why do you think you ought to have a pill?'

'I usually have a pill after lunch. I always have one.' Mouth trembling, Kidney repeated, 'After lunch I have one.'

'Well, I don't know if it does much good really, but if you feel you ought to –' Capitulating, Joseph decided to let Kidney have his pill.

'They said I must.'

'Who're they?'

'My mother's doctor says I must have one after lunch.'

'All right, all right.' Joseph scratched his head not knowing what else to say.

'They said in hospital I should take a pill after lunch,' volunteered Kidney. 'In hospital my mother tried to see me, but she didn't see me. The Government wouldn't let her. Then she came later and I went home. They told me to take my pills three times a day.'

'Don't worry. You'll get your pill.' Joseph went to the wicker basket beneath the settee and pulled it clear. He found the glass bottle. He took out an oblong capsule and replaced the bottle in the wicker basket. 'Here you are,' he said, coming back to the table with the pill.

Kidney swallowed the capsule without water. He seemed anxious to tell Joseph about the hospital. 'It was a big hospital', he said. 'There was a man there ...'

'Oh, yes,' said Joseph.

'He gave me my pills ... He was there when I woke up.'

'In the morning, you mean?'

'He called me sonny.'

'That was friendly.'

'I said I wanted to go home.' Kidney played with a fork left in the centre of the table. 'It was night and the man told me to be quiet.'

'They have rules,' said Joseph.

'The man said: "Be quiet. Do you want a hot thing up you, sonny?".'

Joseph sat still. He felt distressed. Clearing his throat, he had every intention of saying something meaningful, but he merely said. 'You go down to the stream and see Roland. I'll be down when I've washed the dishes.'

It was the disgruntled Willie who saw the smoke. There was a line, black and waving, widening as he watched, rising into the blue sky.

'Great God,' he shouted, running like hell, passing the hut and the curious Joseph standing in the doorway. 'The bloody wood's on fire.' He jumped like a wrestler on all fours into the bracken on the slope. 'It's them damn women of yours,' he told the man at the door, voice shrill, pulling out handfulls of grass and nettles in a frantic attempt to locate the water pipe buried in the ground.

'A fire,' Joseph said calmly, a tea towel draped over his arm. 'Are you sure?'

'Dropping their bloody fags all over my woods.' Willie was too far gone to notice the use of the possessive. He was sitting in the undergrowth now with the pipe between his short legs. 'Come on up, you bastard,' he moaned, wrenching the tap further to the right, spit dribbling down his stubbled chin, his mind shifting from one thought to another, each idea more overlaid than the last, till all he had in his brain was a pattern of leaves, miraculously veined, each one ablaze behind his eyes.

'No good mucking about with water,' observed Joseph. 'I divine Mr George will be in control.' He went at a trot along the path, away from the struggling Willie, and disappeared down the slope.

A little above the stream, the scent of the fire reached him. He forsook the path and plunged down into the ravine, leaping and sliding, adopting a sideways position with arms wildly waving to balance himself. Boots crushing the black ivy that

51

ran like main arteries across the curve of the hillside, he lost his tea towel to a low bush and slithering now on the bare rocks of the lower slopes missed his footing entirely. Guillotining a foxglove with the upward kick of his boot, he rolled clear to the bottom of the incline, coming to a halt finally with his head against the wet clay at the edge of the river, his boots in the thin trickle of water, his fists full of pebbles.

On the opposite bank, a hundred yards up the hillside, Balfour and George were beating the undergrowth with sycamore branches.

Further along the stream, at the bridge, Roland and Kidney heard the stampeding firefighters come down on either side, but saw no one. Roland was busy with his boat, and the reclining Kidney was laid flat on the wooden planks of the bridge, his head stuck out over the edge and his hands folded under his chin, watching the water go over the river bed and the red boat getting nowhere.

Dotty, who had been in the barn when the raised voices had disturbed her, found Willie sitting in the grass.

'What's up, Willie?' she asked, looking down at him, puzzled. His eyes, full of surprise, were fixed on the apex of a bush.

She moved into the bracken and squatted down on her haunches the better to observe him, staring at the freckles thick across the bridge of his lumpy nose. She thought maybe he was drunk. He sat so stiffly, clutching that iron thing sticking up out of the ground. He didn't smell of drink, only of grass and smoke and he looked more baffled than stupefied.

'Willie,' she said, almost afraid, and put her hand on his two clasped ones, stroking the speckled skin upwards to the wrist, fingering his pulse though she didn't know what it might signify, and wishing he would look at her. She tried to remove his hands from around the pipe, and as she struggled he suddenly released his grip and collapsed on his back into the bushes. His cap fell off and he lay there staring up at the sky in that surprised way.

'Willie,' she said again, not very loudly, and stood up and didn't know what to do for the best. Then she ran away down the slope towards the stream, shouting, 'George, George', feeling excited and fearful and important all at the same time.

George told Joseph he'd better bring the Jaguar round to the field road in case Willie needed moving urgently.

'Perhaps it's a stroke,' Balfour suggested. 'It c-could be that by the sound of it.'

'Perhaps,' George said. 'Possibly it's hunger. He's been about since dawn. Still, you'd better go and bring the car round.' Authoritatively he strode up the path towards the stricken Willie with Balfour in pursuit.

'Where are you going?' asked Roland, as his father and Dotty crossed the bridge.

'Just to the car, boy.'

'May I come?' Already the child was scrambling out of the water, boat forgotten.

'No,' Joseph said, not turning round, going very fast up the slope to the Big House. His hands were quite sore – not burnt, possibly blistered from all that sycamore-wielding. His head ached and his eyes hurt. It accelerated him the more. He swung his arms in a fury and leapt up the path.

'Do you think Willie's dead?' Dotty cried, sure he wasn't, but feeling sick as she tried to keep pace with Joseph. It wasn't like Joseph to rush in an emergency. More like, he was running away from her.

'Almost certainly,' he shouted, grinning to himself, holding his smarting hands a fraction before him.

Stubbornly Dotty ran behind him, both of them pursued by a black spiral of gnats.

As they drove up the hill in the Jaguar, a green Mini turned the corner. The narrowness of the lane forced Joseph to slow down. 'Can't stop, old man. Somebody's died on us,' he called and drove on at speed.

'Was that Lionel?' shouted Dotty.

Joseph heard the upward inflection of her provincial voice and found it objectionable. Dotty twisted in her seat in time to see the green Mini halted and lost in the hedge-rimmed lane. At the crossroads Joseph turned right and drove half a mile to the corner shop. She was left sitting in the hot car staring at a border of pinks in the small garden.

Joseph came out of the shop with several bars of chocolate and a tube of cold cream.

'What's wrong with your face?' Dotty asked, looking at the colour of it, glowing red and smudged with black.

He didn't reply, sitting at the wheel smearing grease into the smarting palms of his hands.

'What have you been doing? You're all dirty.'

He reversed the car up the lane, looking over his shoulder as he did so. The breeze blew something from his hair.

'You've got bits of leaves in your hair,' she said, puzzled.

'I've been having it off with old George in the bushes,' he shouted, lips drawn back to show his teeth, and she thought she saw the small endings of his beard shrivelled up in the bright light, as if singed by the sun.

The green Mini was at the crossroads. There was Lionel's elbow in a white sleeve sticking out from the window like a flag of truce. As the Jaguar sped past, Joseph pointed his arm to the sky, spreading his blackened hand against the cool breeze. He didn't turn his head.

Dotty swivelled round and waved at the Mini. 'Not long, not long,' she cried, kneeling in the passenger seat, her hair blowing about her face.

The Jaguar turned into an opening at the side of the lane and stopped in front of a five-barred gate. Lionel turned too, manoeuvring the Mini carefully, and switched off the engine. He let the little silver ignition key dangle between his fingers, sitting there with pleasure and good humour on his flushed face, waiting for Joseph to greet him, his darling wife May safe beside him.

'Glad you made it,' said Joseph, coming to the car. About to shake the hand held out to him, he drew back. 'Sorry, bit of a fire down in the Glen ... Hands a bit sore.' He wiped his cold-creamed hands on the side of his trousers and looked at May. 'Ah, the lovely May. How are you, darling?'

May giggled and stepped out of the Mini in her new pink trews and her gingham shirt, a white silk handkerchief tied casually about her neck. She turned her powdered cheek for Joseph's gallant kiss, moving past Dotty with a jangling of the charm bracelet on her rounded arm and stood at the barred gate looking about her at the view.

Lionel said the Mersey Tunnel hadn't been too crowded. Better than expected, in fact. Dotty hadn't met him before. She thought he was nice, because he shook her hand and said he was glad to meet her. He seemed an unlikely partner for the restless May.

May said how pretty the scenery was. 'So unspoilt and countrified.' She giggled, because she wasn't a fool, and the remarks faded into the summer air as they followed each other over the gate. She very nearly fell on her knees on the far side.

Lionel opened his mouth in alarm. 'Take it easy, my darling,' he cried, attempting to take his wife's arm, but she stepped away from him.

Over the brow of the hill came Balfour and George, carrying an iron bedstead with the body of Willie laid on a striped mattress splotched with damp.

When the two groups met, the bearers halted and lowered the cot to the grass, and Dotty said 'How is he?', looking down at the sunken mouth and the stubbled chin – all that was visible of Willie, for his eyes and nose were covered by his cap.

'I think he's all right ... just a bit dazed. Been overdoing it.' George sat down on the mattress and laid his white fingers on the Welshman's knees. 'Home soon, Willie, home soon.' He hung his head, still touching Willie, and appeared not to see the new arrivals.

May had never seen anyone quite so tall as George. She stood with one hand, the one with the bracelet about her wrist, gripping the bars of the bed, and smiled into the field. Lionel adopted a tragic expression, bending his head low as if in church, though he wasn't sure why there was an old man lying on a bed in a field, and not sure who the tall fellow was or the other shorter one with the spotty complexion. He had understood from Joseph's letter that there would be just Dotty and themselves out in the woods. Of course, Joseph, being arty, was often vague. May had wanted to go abroad, or to a hotel on the coast at least, but he simply couldn't raise the money and he thought it safer to take her somewhere secluded, rather than expose her to the twin temptations of casual acquaintanceships and drink. It was something he often told her. 'Any casual acquaintance could have you in drink. You simply have no sense of responsibility.'

'Is he ill, poor old fellow?' Lionel asked, standing stockily in his good suit with the rather wide trousers and his white stiff collar tight about his neck.

'I believe so,' said Joseph, not interested, wanting to sit down somewhere. He told Dotty, 'I think I ought to go and see about Roland.'

'Ah, Roland.' Lionel jangled pennies in his pocket, remembering the vanishing tricks with money that he had shown Roland a year earlier. 'I'm looking forward to seeing Roland.' He meant it. 'Coming along all right, is he?'

'You've got to drive Willie home in the car,' George said.

'Of course, of course,' Joseph agreed, genuinely ashamed of being so forgetful. He took Balfour's place at the foot of the bed, and he and George carried the stretcher towards the gate. Lionel marched ahead in his shiny brown shoes, anxious to be helpful.

Balfour was astonished by May. She was the living reality of

56

the mound of old dreams dreamt in puberty of fair women coming to lie down beside him. He was fearful to speak lest he should utter obscenities.

Seeing his glance, May, with eyes lavender blue, smiled in his direction, at which he blushed and turned to follow George.

'Isn't he ghastly,' said May, playing with her charm bracelet and looking at Dotty.

'Ghastly?' said Dotty. 'Balfour's not ghastly at all. He's rather interesting. He's very funny when you get to know him. He got tight last night.'

'I mean Lionel, my Lionel. He makes me sick,' said May.

Willie, warm in his womb-world under the covering of his cap, breathed in odours of silk linings and something else, something that was vegetable. He thought he was on his way to the annual hot-pot dinner given by the mine owners for their employees, at the Herbert Arms. He could smell potatoes and gravy, and he was aware of an intense hunger. He could hear the voice of the boss come up from Liverpool in his grand expensive car, the car with the green hood, asking how he was. He struggled to touch the brim of his cap, and his wife was telling him he'd made a fool of himself as usual, or was it his mother? 'Drunk you are, Willie,' she said, but how was a man to resist free drink, dressed in his Sunday suit, brown with a white stripe in it, and the boss making a little speech, standing there on the stone-flagged floor in a pair of plus fours the colour of tobacco, handing them all a cigar and telling them the directors were very pleased with the work done. They dug barytes out of the ground and somewhere along the line it got put into gallons of paint – God knows what it did, though no doubt it made someone a heap of old money. He didn't doubt that. You didn't give close on forty men a hot-pot dinner and as much beer as they could drink, not to mention the cigars and that damn big car with the headlamps shining, unless there was money in it somewhere.

The boss only ever went into the mine once and that was to take his little daughter down, and she put on a white helmet on her head with a candle at the front and all her hair falling down about her shoulders. The little girl used to come to hot-pot do's as well, and each year she got a little taller and her hair a little shorter. He could still hear the rattling of the stall chains as the cows shifted about in the shed in the pub yard. He could almost hear the sound of the men pissing against the wall and see the rivulets of urine running out across the yard. 'Disgusting,' the other folk in the pub called it, but who gave a damn after all that drink, and they wouldn't let them upstairs to use the lav. Couldn't blame them for that. Anyway, the stairs in the pub were waxed like glass, weren't they? There'd have been nothing but broken legs and damaged skulls. There were quite a few breakages as it was. Mugs and the like and one or two plates falling on to the stone floor and old Davis shouting out to be careful of that case of stuffed birds in the corner – a damn big glass case full of birds, like none you ever saw in your life. Coloured like beetles they were, scarlet and blue and bottle-green, all perched on a bit of tree. 'Mind them birds,' Davis would shout. 'Just you be careful of them birds.' Course he had a thing about birds – not live ones at all, but stuffed birds and painted birds on plates. Old Davis had a job to get them out of the pub. Some of them would go right through to the back into the old kitchen and climb up the steps to the loft to sleep the drink off, sleeping up there in the straw with the dog – nice little bitch, that dog – with the sides of bacon hanging up on the beams to remind you flesh was mortal. They were grand times. The men worked hard enough, God only knows, and they did have lonely lives. There seemed one long leap of loneliness from the time they were lads to the nights of the hot-pot suppers. Most of them had been boys in the same school, such as it was – with church twice on Sunday, fishing down at the river, a bit of football in the winter, a couple of outings to Shrewsbury – and then it was all over, and they all went away from each other into houses in the village and took wives and got lads of their own. Then it was as if they'd never been boys at all. Responsible they all were, men they all were, till hot-pot supper night. Everything was different those nights, somehow. There was the church in the daytime you hardly even noticed, grown big as a cathedral with a graveyard like a battlefield, and the ivy climbing up the side of Albert Price's house and Albert at the window with his shotgun telling them all to go to the devil. All the lads stumbling through the churchyard, shouting out to each other like boys, linking arms in the lane and laughing dirty-like seeing the light go on in Mrs Parry's window, knowing old Freddie White was creeping in, like as not, with his boots in his hand. Everyone knowing each other, a funny kind of knowing – though it was a daft way to think, because didn't they still know each other, though some were dead? He was so damn hungry.

He tried to sit up and someone pushed his head down again and he could swear he was lying on the leather seats of the boss's car.

Balfour waited to help Lionel carry his luggage to the huts. He sat on the bed vacated by the delirious Willie and watched Lionel doing things with a dustpan and brush to the interior of the car. Now and then the tidy man would bob his head over the top of the car, his face one big apologetic smile. 'Won't be a tick, old man – just want to get the car spruced up.' May had dropped sweet papers everywhere, and ash from her du Maurier cigarettes, and there was a frosting of face powder on the felt floor-covering beneath the passenger seat.

'The little woman loves her sweeties,' Lionel told Balfour, emerging at last with the dustpan in one hand and brush in the other. About to scatter the contents of the pan into the hedge, he stopped abruptly and said, 'Wrong thing to do, don't you think? Honour the country code and all that.' Contritely he put the pan and brush away in the boot of the car and took out a black leather suitcase and a holdall in

59

tartan cloth. 'Food,' he told Balfour, putting the holdall down on the bed. 'Eggs and stuff.'

They left the gate open for Joseph and George to shut on their return.

'Nothing to get out anyway,' remarked Lionel. They carried the bed at breast height, Lionel's red face smiling through the bars at Balfour walking backwards through the field. 'Not going too fast am I, old chap?'

'No, no it's all right.'

'Marvellous air, marvellous.'

Balfour agreed.

'Been here long?'

'Yes – well, a c-couple of days that is.'

'I see.' Lionel thought perhaps he was shy. It was odd how some people found such difficulty in communicating. He himself had always been able to communicate. His army training, he supposed. Good fellow though, he thought, looking at the marked face and the well-developed shoulders. Salt of the earth, that kind. He prided himself on being a good judge of character. Had to be during the war. Make one mistake in a chap's ability and it could mean a platoon wiped out. The thought bursting out beneath his ginger moustache, he confided: 'Reminds me of the old days, this. In the war, you know. Carrying supplies up to the line. An army marches on its stomach and all that.' Short of breath, sweat dripping into his eyes, he shot a blind glance at his companion. 'Before your time, of course.'

'I never even got to do my National Service,' admitted Balfour.

'Oh, how's that?'

Without waiting for a reply, Lionel puffed on. 'Best training a chap could have, best discipline in the world. Quite indescribable. Seen all types from all walks of life, and – make no bones about it – it separates the wheat from the chaff.'

Balfour was unhappy about the night before them. He hoped somebody would explain to Lionel the sleeping

60

arrangements. Even if Lionel did seem to care for barrack-room life, he would hardly approve of his wife dossing down in the same cubicle as another recruit. Balfour hoped he would take it upon himself to separate the wheat from the chaff and allocate another room to himself and his spouse.

'Ho, there,' Lionel shouted, face scarlet with exertion. They were almost at the hut. 'May, sweetheart.'

Behind his back Balfour heard May reply, 'I'm here, Lionel.' She was leaning against the door of the hut. Through the window Dotty could be seen filling the kettle with water.

'Isn't it marvellous, sweetheart?' asked Lionel, gazing about him at the greenness and the shade.

Lionel spoke the endearment in a natural way. Balfour recognised that. It wasn't just a word tacked on to a sentence that was banal. She was his sweetheart. 'Sweetheart, sweetheart' Lionel would continue to name her when they were alone. But then they weren't going to be alone. He, Balfour, would lie close to them. 'Making tea, Dotty,' he called, unable to go into the hut for the upward swell of May's breasts and the perfume that covered her like a cloak.

At that moment Lionel, as if overcome by the quality of the air and the scenery about them, ran away from his sweetheart in the doorway and went hopping towards the trees, his brown shoes dancing under the leaves and a white moon of baldness, not previously seen, rising across the slopes of his ginger head. Sounds came from him like an elephant trumpeting.

'Goodness,' May said and went into the hut, perhaps in disgust, leaving only Balfour to see Roland running straight into Lionel's arms. The child was swung into the air and down again and held against the grandfatherly moustache and kissed and borne with gusto and hilarity back to the hut and up the steps.

'Look what I've found,' Lionel said archly, holding Roland like a baby.

'Hallo, Roland,' said May.

'I've found a Roland, and such a big Roland. My word he's

a big Roland.' The big Roland was swung upwards again to the ceiling. 'Too big for tricks now ... much too big, aren't you?'

'He'll be sick if you keep doing that,' May told him.

'Not big Roland ... not our big Roland ... Oh, dear no. No fear of that.' Lionel was loth to put his playmate down. He held him in his arms and glowed with pride and tenderness.

'I didn't know you were coming,' Roland said. 'Nobody said you were coming.'

May sat smiling at the boy and the man, tapping her tinted nails against the surface of the table, not caring whether they had been expected or not. She'd told Lionel he was a fool to write to Joseph. She'd told him, hadn't she, that it was just one of those invitations thrown out after a few drinks and never intended to be taken seriously. And who the hell wanted to spend a couple of weeks right out in the country miles away from the shops and things? It wasn't as if they were friends of Joseph's. She knew him from the old days in Liverpool, and that fat wife of his and Dotty too – but Lionel hadn't really known them. He was almost a stranger, and God knows they had nothing in common. It was just a silly statement made after a few drinks. She had rebelled at being taken to Kew to look at the bamboo or cactus, or whatever they were, and had demanded they go somewhere for a drink – not the Cumberland or the Mayfair Hotel or anywhere where she felt lost, but a proper pub – and somehow they had ended up in the North Star on the Finchley Road. There they'd bumped into Joseph and Dotty. Lionel had said, in that delighted way he affected, 'Why, look who's here', and May had had to stop and smile, though she felt more like screaming, and the four of them sat on those stools that she hated because they made you feel so insecure and lopsided, and talked utter inanities. Lionel stood them all drinks, of course, which he couldn't afford, and just before they were going Joseph said 'We must meet again soon', and Lionel, the idiot, said, 'Oh yes, when?' And so on, until finally Joseph said, 'Why don't you both come down to

Wales with me? We Northerners ought to stick together.'

Afterwards in the car May had told Lionel what a fool he was, what an exhibition he had made of himself. 'Couldn't you see that Joseph was bored stiff with everything you said?' she told him. 'Couldn't you see he was yawning his head off?' Lionel had just turned to her at the traffic lights with those reproachful eyes and asked if she was feeling tired, if her monthlies were on the way. 'Sweetheart,' were his words, 'you know you're due for your monthlies. Don't hurt me.' He knew more about her monthlies, as he called them, than she did herself. Not that there was any danger of her 'monthlies' not being due – not the kinky way Lionel behaved. How she fought him, how she wasted her time trying to goad him and wound him. It just never got through to him – he was encased in armour. It was stupid really, because all the time she was screaming at him she did know fractionally that he was good and sincere and normal – yes, even normal in a way – and that he was light years away from people like Joseph, superior in every way. Yet she couldn't tell him. She hated him for his rolling belly and the bald patch on his head and the way he would go on about the army, and deep down, way way down, she was frightened of him and of what he thought of her. He didn't even know her, and she couldn't explain herself how she had come to marry this stranger with the thinning hair.

When she was a child her mother had told her that she was utterly beautiful, perfectly formed, and that men would love her for her skin alone. Her mother said she would marry a prince of men with a private income, and here she was at the end with a skin still flawless and a husband with a pot belly and a nostalgia for the war. She pretended not to know about the war, but she did know. While Lionel had stripped down his Bren gun and led his men across Italy (she knew the route as well as he now), she had been a child following her father from camp to camp across England. In the married quarters her mother had tucked her up in the army-issue blankets and commented on her lovely skin. But despite her complexion, she had ended up with Lionel. She had met him in a cinema and he had taken her home in his Triumph Herald. She had been impressed by his manners and by his treatment of her. She felt secure with him. It didn't matter if her mascara dribbled down her cheek or her hair came out of set, because she could tell he adored her – and why shouldn't he with his terrible stomach and his hair gone thin and that comical moustache all wet from kissing? So they were married, and the Triumph Herald disappeared, and they had to leave the Bayswater flat, and then the Maida Vale one, and then one after that. He still said he was going to cover her with jewels. 'You'll be worth £3,000 standing up,' he'd told her, fondling what he called her 'chests' and pressing his moustache against her nose.

He still promised her things. He still went out daily and returned at six o'clock to tell her his shares were looking up – they always looked down the following day. He lectured her on her personal hygiene and put up with all her cruelties and abuse and disloyalty. When he came in at night he took off his good suit and changed into his pyjamas and sat on the sofa while she made a cup of tea. It was the extent of her wifely duties. He changed so as not to crumple his suit. His feet stuck out and his neck was marked at the throat by his collar stud. She only wanted him to touch her when he was dressed as the business executive he pretended to be. She could take the caresses of the man of the Stock Exchange, soon to make his million, but she despised the tubby husband panting on the mohair settee in the expensive flat with the yellow brocade curtains and the plastic tulips on the windowsill. He never made jokes, he never tried to fight back at her. There was no fun and no victory in hitting a man who so pitifully lay down. He made her wear dresses with high necks and complained that she deliberately wore her skirts too short, and he wouldn't let her see her old friends. He followed her round like a hospital nurse, plumping up cushions behind her head and washing out her nylons and cleaning her shoes. 'In the army,'

64

he told her, 'you got to realise what cleanliness was. It's just not on to polish only the tops of your shoes. The instep also must be shone.' He'd done it in the trenches apparently – those Italian trenches – to set an example to his men. He'd made an effort to shave before consuming his tins of bully beef or whatever, because 'it's the little things that make a gentleman'. Even his war wound had been ridiculous. A piece of shrapnel from a shell scored through the ample flesh of his bottom. 'Did it hurt?' she had asked him idly, thinking of him clutching his behind on the road to Rome.

He would prepare their evening meal in his pyjamas and arrange it daintily on a tray. Then they watched the telly, and he sat her on his knee and began to whisper those things into her ear, never realising how incongruous was the change from Gentleman Jim in the trenches to Dirty Dick on the rented settee, as he mouthed those dreadful words into her brain as if he were demented. She didn't altogether dislike it. There was a certain thrill to be experienced. It did make her feel she wasn't entirely living out her life in a wicker basket under a barrage baloon floating high above the rest of the world. If only he would call her May instead of Sweetheart, if only he would give her a name. 'What will I be worth lying down?' she would ask him brutally, as he foraged in the whorl of her ear, and he would moan, 'Sweetheart, sweetheart, how I love you. How you love me.'

'Sweetheart,' said Lionel, placing the child on the floor, 'I've brought your cigarettes.' He handed her the packet with a tender smile. Dotty put cups on the table and Balfour stared out of the doorway. Presently he said 'Roland, there's your Dad', and the child ran out into the sunlight and across the field.

'Who,' asked May, 'is that huge lad wearing the football scarf?'

'It's George,' Dotty said, making the tea. 'George MacFarley, who owns these woods – him and his parents.'

65

'It's probably glandular,' May remarked, beginning to open her cigarette packet and watching Lionel's hand go to the pocket of his suit for his lighter. Deliberately she put the packet down again.

'It's nothing glandular,' said Balfour. 'H-his father and his uncle are very tall men. Broad too. They both look like gods. When he grows a bit, he'll be l-like them.'

May laughed and Balfour bent down to scratch at his ankle. He hadn't actually looked at her face yet. He daren't. She was pink and white like a carnation, and heavy with scent.

The two women began a conversation that was incomprehensible to him.

'That tall one who gave us a lift –' said Dotty.

'The one you liked –'

'The one *you* liked –'

May chose to deny this emphatically. 'I hated him. I told him so. He wore bicycle clips.'

'He never. Not the tall one.'

'In the Hope Hall. You said he was nice and I said he was awful.'

George and Joseph entered the hut and Dotty poured out more tea. She was relieved to see Joseph making an effort to be polite to Lionel, shaking him by the hand and introducing him to George.

May took out a cigarette and said 'Might I have a light, Lionel', and he replied 'Sweetheart, sweetheart' and was ashamed of himself for having to be asked. He hadn't noticed that she wanted a light – he had been too busy being introduced to the tall fellow. He had thought she needed a light several minutes earlier before that odd conversation about the Hope Hall. Sounded like something to do with the Salvation Army. It wasn't like May to accept lifts from strangers. Anyway, she seemed to have hated him, whoever he was. She'd said twice she'd hated him. He hoped it was a long time ago.

George and Lionel, surprisingly, had a lot to say to each other. George wanted to know if he had been to Palestine. Lionel had. He was there in 1946. Had he been to Cyprus? There too. George sat stiffly in his rocking chair, his hands still black from the fire, folded in his lap. His slanted eyes, shining and mournful, shifted from the army man with the little brown moustache to the green field beyond the hut, and back again.

Losing himself down a maze of streets with exotic names, some mispronounced, Lionel named comrades and regiments, gave his impressions and his opinions, his head inclined solemnly.

After a while Joseph took Roland by the hand and left the hut. May and Dotty went into the barn and May combed out her hair in front of the mildewed mirror. 'What on earth is there to do round here?' she asked peevishly.

'It's not too bad, love. The thing is, the air knocks you out and you sleep a lot.' Dotty remembered where May was to spend her nights. She said, 'You know Balfour, the one with the pimples, the one that can't look you in the eye – well, you and Lionel are sharing a hut with him.'

'A hut? Really.' May didn't care. She asked spitefully, 'Still not married to Joseph?'

'You know damn well I'm not,' said Dotty.

May said, trying to be nice, 'Anyway, you're better off than I am with my Lionel. He's a fool.'

'I think he loves you.'

May shrugged her shoulders, doing things now to her eyelashes, spitting on a little brush to moisten the mascara, blinking rapidly at the mirror. 'I don't know what he thinks. I don't even know what I'm doing here.' Her mouth sagged wider as she worked at the splayed lashes and she leaned forward to see her reflection more closely.

It's true, Dotty thought, and was frightened. She said, 'I don't know either. Honest to God, isn't it awful?' Frowning

67

dreadfully, shoulders hunched, she paced up and down behind the titivating May. 'It's all so silly … this love business.'

'I never tell Lionel I love him. I don't think one should.' May looked critically at her reflection. 'Lionel cut all the stuffing out of my bras, you know.'

'What for?'

'God knows. He does all sorts of funny things. You wouldn't believe it. All about how he'll kill me with a karate blow to my womanhood, and all that stuff about the army. You just wait till he takes you on one side and tells you about his coin.'

'His what?' asked Dotty.

'It's a coin he keeps on a chain round his neck,' May said. 'He pretends it's very special and private, and he tells everyone about it at the drop of a hat. It's supposed to be valuable and dreadfully historical, and it's really a metal token for one penny issued by the Blakeley Moor Co-op in 1827. God knows where he got it. It looks ridiculous when he hasn't got his shirt on. He's never without it, never.'

'Does he wear it in the bath?' Dotty saw him fox-coloured beneath the water, the Blakeley Moor coin moving gently across his primitive chest.

'He keeps saying I'll be worth £3,000 lying down.'

They both started to laugh – Dotty loudly, with her mouth wide open and her two feet set in a circlet of sunshine. May with pink lips compressed and shoulders wriggling.

68

5

Roland went to bed that evening without complaining. For one thing Lionel had played with him in the field after supper – the sunset field with everything cool and the darkness growing. The trees flapped like rags. When Lionel pushed him high on the swing the air rushed at his sunburnt face, its chillness covering his bare arms with goose pimples. He dropped from the swing and ran round and round the hut, screaming with excitement as the fat man chased him, until he flew into a patch of bramble and lacerated his leg. He bent his head and watched the blood beading on the surface of his leg. Lionel held his ankle in one big hand and dabbed at the scratch with his handkerchief, transferring the three pin-points of blood on to the white square of cloth. Even as Roland looked, his disappointed mouth open, the spots of redness reappeared again. He scrambled free of the man's hand and ran about the field triumphantly, shouting for Lionel to catch him. 'Catch me, catch me,' he cried, falling into the long grass with his flushed face close to the cooling earth and his leg forgotten. The other thing that made going to bed so pleasant was the two-shilling piece Lionel had found in his ear. Lionel had sat him on the table among the dirty dishes and magicked his toothbrush into the biscuit tin on the draining board. 'Dotty, Dotty,' he had said, 'see if Roland's toothbrush is in the biscuit tin.' And Dotty had got up from her chair and Lionel had said 'Go on, go on, find Roland's toothbrush', and Dotty opened the biscuit tin and indeed his toothbrush was there. 'Aaaaaahya-ya,' said his father, yawning, champing his lips together and trapping pieces of his beard. And then Lionel had placed his hands about Roland's head and touched his ears and neck, till he squirmed on the table top and laughed and nearly upset the plates, and Lionel said, 'What's this in Roland's ear?' His probing fingers tickled his right ear, and he wriggled still more because everything about Lionel was so warm and friendly – the warm breath coming out of his mouth, the little coloured moustache quivering, and his face smiling, smiling. And there was the two-shilling piece: a silver coin, two shillings in one, an old one with a King's head on, not the picture of the Queen sitting on her horse. 'A two-shilling piece in Roland's ear,' Lionel had shouted. 'All for Roland. Finding's keepings.' May had given a small laugh as if she thought it was funny, which it was, and Joseph had yawned again and said at the end of it, 'Come on, boy. Bed for you.' Off he went, still feeling the prickles of Lionel's moustache against his ear, the silver money clutched tight in his hand – a lot of money, though of course he knew there wasn't any more to be found like that, not in his ear or up his nose or anywhere. It wasn't really magic. There was an explanation. But he was drowsy and he slipped from his father's arms like a fish being loosed in the sea. He fell asleep at once.

Lionel was a domestic asset. Without him they would all have sat half stupefied in the nearly dark hut. He washed the supper dishes and refilled the bowl with soapy water and washed out the tea towel, rinsing it carefully and going out into the field to hang it over a bush to dry. He even found a stiff brush and swept crumbs into a small heap at the door. 'Ha, ha, ha,' he went, swinging his brush like a golfer, sending a half crust of bread out into the dusk and humming little snatches of songs. Finally he stood in the open doorway and took great gulps of night air. 'This is the life,' he cried, expanding his chest, his eyes glowing with happiness. 'This is the life.' He needed May to confirm his opinion. 'Isn't this the life? Isn't it, sweetheart?' he demanded, turning to her.

'Oh, do sit down,' she told him, annoyed. She caught Balfour looking at her in the gloom.

Joseph fetched the paraffin lamp from the far end of the hut and lit it. A moth flew in through the open window and dashed itself against the lamp. May shuddered and fluttered her hands in horror. Lionel protected her at once – big protective Lionel. His handkerchief dropped the insect to the table. 'Don't be concerned,' he said. 'It will not harm you.' Balfour, startled by the sudden flourish of white calico that had stunned the moth, heard the words and finished the sentence in his head, the verse of the song ... 'It's only me pursuing something I'm not sure of ...' He knew two popular songs and those not very well. The 'Don't be concerned' one and 'Talking about my generation', written it seemed deliberately to parody his own affliction. He didn't know every word like the lads in the club, but certain lines of each song remained engraved on his mind –

'Hope I die before I get old ...
Talking about my g-generation ...
Don't want to be a big s-sensation,
Why don't you all f-fade away ...'

Dotty was lifting the Monopoly box out from beneath the sofa. 'Might we?' she asked Joseph, sure she would be refused.

But Joseph welcomed the idea. He clapped his blistered hands together and said loudly, 'Come on, let's play Monopoly. Do you good, George.'

George, furthest from the table, said nothing. He had been thinking about Willie, the coffin shape his body had assumed as they carried him feet first through the doorway of his cottage. He thought about the fire too, the possible cause of it. Apart from Willie, only Dotty smoked; but then she had been in the barn or down at the stream most of the time. Willie must have passed that way earlier in the day; it could only

71

have been him. In all those years he had never been careless. But there was always a first time. George would have liked to know what Joseph was thinking about at this moment as he sat with his hands busy with the bundles of artificial money and his head constantly jerking backwards to flick away the falling lock of hair.

Lionel, laughing in anticipation – it was years since he had played Monopoly – fetched chairs from the dim corners of the hut and grouped them about the table. He had tried to talk to Kidney at supper and failed. He realised that the boy wasn't altogether there. In an attempt to show that he felt that no blame should be attached to him, he constantly smiled and winked at the unresponsive lad. He sat himself on the wooden bench and patted the space beside him.

'Ever played before?' he asked, expecting no reply, ready to cover up the silence with a cough or a laugh or a squeeze at the waist of the drowsing May.

'Yes, indeed,' Kidney said, and sat heavily down on the wooden bench, his curved thighs trapped under the edge of the solid table, his voice deep with comprehension.

May, apathetic with country air and boredom, remained where she was, seated opposite the perspiring Balfour. She remembered now that Dotty never went anywhere without her game of Monopoly. In the old days in Liverpool they had played it often. Sometimes it went on for hours and hours. Absolutely endless. Enjoyment depended entirely on who was playing. There was no hope tonight, she thought, looking with amusement at the players about the board, the uncomfortable Balfour and the snooty Joseph, not to mention potty Kidney – or whatever his name was. What on earth was he doing here? She must ask Dotty. Not that it really mattered. She could ask herself the same question and receive an equally unsatisfying reply.

Joseph was offering the two women a choice of symbols.

'Do you want the boat, the train, the shoe, the car, the hat, the dog, or the iron?' he asked them, touching the little metal objects with his finger. He himself always had the train.

'Oh dear!' May exclaimed, wanting a nice hot bath.

'Come on, make up your mind.' Impatiently Joseph pushed the iron towards her with the tips of his burnt fingers.

'I hate ironing.' Childishly May turned down the corners of her mouth, and Lionel said soothingly, 'So you do, my sweetheart ... Poor little sweetheart.'

Balfour chose the car, but after a moment Joseph took it away from him and gave him the dog. Kidney, it seemed, usually had the car. Reassured, Kidney held it upright on the palm of his hand and smiled down upon it. 'Once,' he told Lionel, 'I won. That's a fact, isn't it Joseph?'

It was a true claim. Once, in the early days, to give him confidence, they had let him win. Joseph had never asked for rent when the youth landed on his property, and Dotty had kept telling him that the bank owed him money.

While Joseph laid out the property cards according to value and colour, Lionel reminisced aloud about his Monopoly days.

'In Brighton, long before the war,' he told them, 'when the family was at home. It all comes back to me now.' Its coming suffused his face with a glow of pleasure. 'We used to play on the billiard table, on a sheet of course – myself and father and Alice and George and Hetty ... after supper on a Sunday, all the family round the table.'

'On the billiard table?' May winked at Dotty and ran the little iron up and down the pale board. 'Must have been a big house, Lionel.'

'Quite big,' he said modestly. 'Quite big, my sweetheart. Remember? I showed it you once.'

He had driven her to Brighton one afternoon in the summer, and they had spent a perfectly vile afternoon listening to the band. Not a soul under ninety anywhere around. 'I might,' she told him tartly, 'be prepared to do this sort of thing in the twilight of our life, but not now.' He had taken her down the road past the house the family had lived in. It might have been the house. It might not. He actually had tears in his eyes as he drove, though it could have been the lingering effect of the military airs the band had played so loudly. He said there was a big garden at the back. You couldn't see it from the road. Take his word for it, it was as big as a field. Mother had been very fond of gardening; and they had played badminton in the summer. He talked about it at length. The white shuttlecock was like a little feathered bird plopping over the net on the warm summer evenings. Mother brought them long glasses of lemonade. Father kept the score. Ridiculous.

'Highest scorer starts,' said Joseph, giving a last tidy touch to his row of cards and throwing the dice.

It did draw them together – the counting of the money, the excitement of landing on Community Chest. Dotty won ten pounds in a beauty contest and they smiled at her and clapped their hands. Even May clapped. 'Quite right, quite right,' Lionel cried, throwing the dice so hard it flew from the table and going in search of it on all fours, his mutilated posterior raised high, laughter dribbling from his mouth. On the return journey he tickled Joseph's leg and was kicked. Both men were convulsed with laughter.

Balfour dared to speak directly to May. She landed on Mayfair and made no move to buy it.

Joseph said she was a fool. 'It's the most valuable property on the board.'

'Is it really?' she asked, fluttering her eyelashes, feeling she was being delightfully vague. 'Well, can I buy it now?'

'No, it's my turn.'

'Hard luck,' Balfour said softly, smiling at her. She shrugged her shoulders at him and giggled.

'I wasn't thinking,' she told him alone.

Joseph managed to acquire Bond Street, Regent Street and Oxford Street. He stopped the game while he bought houses, one on each street. 'Now,' he told them, 'Now, watch out, children.'

74

Dotty bought the Strand, and Lionel protested that it wasn't fair – that he had Trafalgar Square. 'It's not on,' he shouted. 'It's just not on.' She pretended to be spiteful and told him several times she wasn't going to let him get his hands on the Strand, not if he offered her £500 for it.

'Willie cleaned out the lavatory, did he?' asked George suddenly. He had bought nothing and hardly seemed to grasp the point of the game.

'Yes, I believe he did.'

'It wasn't necessary.' George was looking stern. He held the dice in his hand and stared at the board.

'Come on, man. Throw the bloody dice. You're holding up the game.'

George threw.

'It's a chemical toilet of course?' Lionel wanted to know, lowering his voice.

'Did you give him any money?' asked George.

'Didn't have time,' Joseph said. 'Smelt the fire and that was that.'

Kindly, Dotty told Lionel that it was a chemical toilet.

'Well, don't give him any money next time you see him. My father sees to that.' George put his elbows on the table and cupped his head in his hands, letting his eyes close behind the railings of his fingers.

Lionel said, 'I'll take care of the toilet paper. I'm used to that sort of thing.'

The corners of his wife's mouth trembled. She put the back of her hand against her lips, observed by the spying Balfour.

'It's a question of careful planning ... Taking that every man functions normally and performs once a day for seven days, that's four sheets per person, times ...' Lionel counted the group around the table, stabbing the air with one large finger ...' times six – no seven, mustn't forget myself.' He shook with merriment, licked at his moustache, controlled himself and continued ... 'Twenty-eight sheets per day, times seven ...'

75

'Only four sheets per man?' said Joseph mildly.

'Oh shut up, Lionel, shut up and don't be so disgusting.' May couldn't bear it. How dare he talk about her going to the lavatory once a day for seven days in that revolting way. It was both presumptuous and nauseating. 'You're revolting,' she cried, clenching her fists and banging them down so hard on the table that one of Joseph's little green houses fell over.

'Steady on. Mind the bloody board.'

'Forgive me, sweetheart.' Lionel attempted to pat her knee under the brim of the table. 'You had to know that sort of thing in the war, sweetheart –'

'The war, the war,' she mimicked, and two lines appeared on either side of her stretched wide mouth and she turned her profile to Balfour, poking her head forward angrily on its quite short neck, pecking at the still spluttering Lionel, telling him he was a fool, an utter fool. 'You're grotesque, Lionel ... You're utterly grotesque ...'

Lionel flung up his arms, pretending fear, cowering back on his wooden bench, hunched against the stolid Kidney. 'Kamerad,' he said ... 'Kamerad.'

'Going on about your disgusting toilet drill and your dreary war ... Who the hell cares about what you did in the army ... Who do you think you are? D'you know,' she added, turning her attention to Joseph, 'D'you know what he told me on my wedding night?' Her head tossed indignantly, and the shadow of her hair trembled across the Monopoly board. 'He actually told me how to dismantle a Bren gun.'

'Very useful,' Joseph said, not bothering to look at her.

She giggled. Joseph always made her laugh, even if he was so affected.

Lionel mistakenly guffawed his relief. Instantly he aroused fresh resentment.

'You find it funny, do you?' said May. 'You think that funny, you big fat bore?'

'Flattery will get you nowhere, May,' ventured Joseph.

Lionel turned his beaming face from his wife to Joseph and back again. His voice sounded full of tears as he tried to extricate himself. 'Sweetheart, sweetheart, it's not ...'

'Stop calling me sweetheart. Stop it.' She could have wrenched the nose from his face in her anger. Indeed her hand, with the diamond ring encircling the pad of her fourth finger, flew upwards from her lap towards him.

'Sweetheart,' he cried, leaning away from her.

'Joseph has brought six toilet rolls with him,' Kidney said slowly, 'It ought to be enough.' His morello lips stayed open as he tried to remember how many sheets of paper he had used. He quite liked Lionel with his wish to be helpful about the lavatory. They all ought to be responsible for something.

Two spots of colour burned on either cheek of the weakened May. Her eyes under the thick lashes, shone. Her mascara had smudged, giving her face a bruised appearance. They were all fools. They made her sick. She looked sideways at her husband and inconsistently found him less foolish than the others.

Lionel fingered his moustache, as if to reassure himself that it grew on him and wasn't pasted to his lip. How she abused him. How he loved her.

'On no account,' George said, 'must you give Willie any money, Joseph. You mustn't tip him. You do understand that, don't you?' He hoped Joseph did understand, did realise the power money had to corrupt.

Joseph thought he heard crying outside the hut. He went to the door, opened it and listened. A sound like the sea rolled over the dark field towards him. He held up his hand behind him for silence, tilting his head.

'It's the wind,' Dotty said.

He trod carefully across the grass to the side of the barn, leaning his face against the wooden planks at the point just under the window. The wood was still warm from the day's sun, and he raised his eyes above the black shapes of the trees and saw a small moon, the colour of a lemon, dragged by clouds across the sky. Moons, he thought, were so that men like himself would know they lived on earth. He fluttered his arms in the wind, imitating the branches all about him, and

77

wheeled across the grass, smiling, entering the narrow doorway sideways with one arm stretched high, almost to the ceiling, casting a long shadow over the group at the table, so that May shrieked in alarm.

The game went on and on. The little metal objects were moved round and round the squares. No one took any notice of Kidney. He threw the dice and counted his spaces but was never fined. Time and again he landed on a row of red hotels bought by Joseph, and once he said, 'Do I owe you any money, Joseph?' and Joseph replied, 'What? Money? No, shouldn't think so. Your go next, George.' Kidney withdrew into himself, because he knew the rules of the game and he knew he was playing alone.

May was out first. She said 'Thank God', and shortly after Balfour followed, and then Lionel. Lionel put the kettle on and May sat slumped behind the brass paraffin lamp and yawned and yawned. While waiting for the water to boil, Lionel went outside into the field. May could hear him out there under the moon, flooding the grass, and she snapped her mouth shut in the middle of a yawn, and water seeped out of her smudged eyes and the mascara spread across her cheeks. Lionel returned with a fleck of hair curled rakishly about one ear. He ran the tap at the sink and rinsed his hands noisily. Unable to find the tea towel, he took out his useful handkerchief and dried his fingers one by one, pushing back the cuticles of his nails. Looking up, he saw his wife's besmeared face in the lamplight. He came towards her with his forefinger embedded in a damp sheath of material and bent over her, wiping at the stained skin beneath her eyes. She made no resistance. Amusement and anger had long since drained away leaving her detached and apathetic. 'There, there,' he crooned tenderly, cradling her chin in his fingers, making his wife's dirty little face clean and wholesome once more. He put away his soiled handkerchief and rubbed his hands together boyishly, a job well done, telling Balfour it was a grand night. 'A grand night,' he said, with his brown-suited

78

back to the table and his still moist hands holding the tea pot beneath the cold water tap. 'A grand night, a lovely moon. You used to get those sorts of nights in Italy ¬ during the war, you know. There were cypress trees of course, but the same old moon.' He cleared his throat, regretting instantly his mention of the forbidden subject. He couldn't help himself, the best of him had lived through the war. He simply had no notion of himself before 1939. Though he talked to May about Father and his brothers and sisters, he couldn't be sure that his memories were exact. It was as though he were chronicling the recollections of someone he had known, but never intimately. This person had played badminton, he was certain, and there were those holidays in Eastbourne. Like a photograph shown to him, there was Father in a blazer, his trousers rolled above his knees, planted on the shore with the sea showing between his bow legs. He didn't deliberately mean to falsify his rememberings of the time before the war. It was just that one had to play fair by the past. There was a certain code – honour thy father and thy mother and all that. It couldn't have been easy for Father supporting a large family on a bank clerk's pay, though food was cheaper then, and if he'd been strict and tyrannical with the girls and mother it was doubtless with the best of intentions. It wasn't for Lionel to judge. He had a great respect for father – did have – a grand man in many ways. He must have been. Anyway, Father had long since passed on. Lionel had been back several times to Brighton to look at the grave. Once only he brought flowers, and each time it occurred to him that it was a very small grave for such a stern and strong man to spend his time in. The flowers when he next saw them had turned black. The headstone gave his full name, William Robert Gosling, making no mention of the word 'father' at all. In some ways the omission shocked him almost as much as the decayed blossoms. It was as if Father were denying their kinship, as if Father was saying they'd never met.

He smiled, standing at the sink, trying to picture himself in the early days of the war. His hand slipped between the buttons of his shirt to touch the coin hanging there on a chain about his neck. Curious, that incident. He had been in some public urinal in Yorkshire in 1939, without a penny to his name, not even the price of a cup of tea. He saw the coin glinting through the water. It had cost him something, mentally, to do what he had to do, reaching down to retrieve it.

If May could only know how his experience of the world protected her. The world was a deep deceptive forest, full of promises and little glades and clearings, and in the dark depths roamed the wolves, savage, snapping their great teeth, waiting to spring on those who wandered from the path. May was so unaware of the dark places, so trusting, so unconscious of danger. He had to watch for both of them. In the darkness of the world she was a little flower, glowing like a star, beautiful as a pair of little eyes. Sweetheart! How her eyes gleamed. She might now find it boring to be guarded by him, but she was only a child. One day she would tell him that she understood, that she realised what it was he protected her from. She might fret, she might argue with him, but it was only to impress Joseph. He had met Joseph's sort in the war. Different conditions of course, but the basic problem was the same: lack of backbone, deficiency of guts, absence of moral fibre. Those chaps were always the first to find the local brothel, always the first to get a dose of the clap. One or two of that sort in a platoon and the general standard went for a burton. A grand platoon, old Whitey Briggs had told him. 'First class, my boy. I'm proud of you. But I don't altogether care for your V.D. rates.'

May thought that the only way to live was to throw oneself into the depths. He could tell her a few things about that – he'd done so – but she became irritated. The war, the war, she would cry impatiently, not realising that the army dealt with destruction and death and disgust, trained a man to stay upright instead of falling on all fours like an animal among the carnage. And life was war, in a more subtle form, that lasted

80

for ever, and only discipline and careful entrenchment would see you through until your own great Armistice Day. He would see May safely through the lines, even if he had to carry her, kicking her little shoes off on the way.

Such emotion rose up inside his breast that he thought he would break out weeping, and he ran the water into the metal basin and blinked back the tears of love, love fulfilled – for she did love him, he knew – and he cleared his throat again. He was suddenly reminded of a poem. He just had to tell them.

'The moon like a ghostly galleon,
Set in a silver sea ...'

He couldn't find the next line. 'D'you know it?' he asked Balfour, who was getting spoons out of a drawer.

'S-set in a s-silver sea,' repeated Balfour, discomfited. 'I d-don't think I do.'

'Grand poem, grand.' He went out again into the blackness to fetch the tea towel from the blackthorn bush, and they heard him fall heavily and the short splatterings of his good-humoured laughter as he rolled about the alien field. He reappeared, hopping about the table on one leg, spitting through his military moustache, whimpering that he'd broken his leg. He was so boisterous, so full of fun. He made them all feel half dead.

'For God's sake,' May pleaded. Hurriedly Lionel composed himself, dabbing at his drooling mouth with his sleeve and wrapping the tea towel about his hand like a bandage to lift the steaming kettle from the calor gas cooker. He couldn't contain himself. It was so exhilarating out there under the racing clouds and the far-away moon. He had to tell Balfour the other poem he'd remembered. He had to.

'I must go down to the sea again
To the lonely sea and the sky,
And all I ask is a tall, a tall ship,
And a star to –'

81

'Mary in the garden sifting cinders,' interrupted Joseph, rattling the dice in its little cardboard funnel and emptying them across the table. 'Lifted up her skirt – two fours – and farted like a man. The force of the explosion broke fifteen winders, and the clappers of her arse went bang, bang, bang.'

There it was, thought Lionel, sniggering with the rest of them – the hatred of womankind, the wish to defile. 'It's a bit not on in the company of ladies,' he said, knowing he would be ridiculed but compelled to speak.

'You're priceless,' his wife told him, giving little whoops of resurrected joy behind the paraffin lamp.

'It's not that I'm a prude,' he said, 'I could cap that if I cared. Indeed I could.'

'Go on then,' May goaded. 'Go on, St. Lionel.' Not that he was a prude! How fantastic he was. Obscene was the word for him, with his sick sagas of the temple. 'Tell one of your very own stories,' she said daringly, sitting up straight in her chair. But he failed to take her meaning. He simply didn't think she could mean the histories he whispered in her ear when they lay together in bed.

'I-I know a story,' Balfour said, 'A rhyme that is.'

'Go on,' encouraged May, though she detested dirty jokes. Balfour began to recite:

'There was an old Jew of Belgrade
Who kept a dead whore in a cave.
He said I admit
I'm a b-bit of a –'

'Why Jew?' asked George, raising his head and fixing his censorious eyes on Balfour.

'It's just a joke,' apologised Balfour lamely, glad that he had been interrupted. He had forgotten George's preoccupation with the Jews and his interest in Israel. It was just another example of how far short he fell of the high degree of sensitivity attributed to him by Mr and Mrs MacFarley. He supposed he could have said 'There was an old *Scot* of Belgrade', but it was too late for that now. Ashamed of his blunder, he helped the gentlemanly Lionel with the tea-making, putting cups ready on the draining board.

'Go on, George,' shouted Joseph, 'Pull your finger out ... You're in gaol, man. You can't come out yet.' Spooning sugar into his mug, he kept a watchful eye on the unwilling player.

Stubbornly, Kidney played alone, counting his moves and collecting his money from the bank at Joseph's elbow. Beyond the amber circle of the lamplight Balfour and Lionel dissolved into the darkness. Lionel could hardly bear to look at his sweetheart, so beautiful had she become, so luminous in the wooden hut amid the trees. Emotionally he stared at her dewy mouth, slack with tiredness. When she had drunk her tea she stretched herself and told Lionel she wanted to go to bed.

'Sweetheart, of course,' he cried, leaping into the lamplight, his little moustache trembling.

George said he would show them to their hut.

'But you're not out,' protested Joseph.

'I don't want to play any more,' George said, standing up and looking away from the board.

'Well, don't take the lamp.' Joseph put his hand about its base in annoyance. 'The wind would only blow it out.'

'Perhaps,' George said. He opened the door and looked out into the blowing night.

Joseph reluctantly left the table to wave the departing players from the hut, holding the lamp in the doorway and smiling fiercely in the yellow light. Balfour, walking sideways to gesture to the friendly Dotty, was blinded by a sudden gust of wind that blew the hair into his eyes. When he looked again, the door had closed and clouds flew above the roof of the hut.

May hung on to her husband's jacket, shivering with cold. 'It's freezing,' she said, hating the whirling trees and the unseen path. Lionel removed his coat and covered her shoulders. His white shirt glowed in the field ... 'There, there, sweetheart. ... There, there.'

83

'It's like winter,' she wailed, lowering her bleached head and pushing it against his shrapnel-ploughed buttocks, her two arms wrapped about his waist, the man's jacket trailing about her uncertain feet.

'It's quite light, sweetheart,' he told her, seriously endangered by the way she clung to him and worried about his good coat being trampled underfoot. Like a milkmaid with her cheek pressed to the warm flank of a particularly restless cow, she slithered down the path under the wild trees. Small stones stubbed her exposed toes in their absurd sandals. She screamed thinly at regular intervals. Balfour, following behind the joined and lurching couple, couldn't become accustomed to the sound. On each occasion he started and trembled as if a screech owl had flown in his face.

At the hut George said he would fetch the storm lantern from his bedroom for them. Lionel began to thank him profusely. 'Most kind of you, old man ... Much appreciated ... The little woman doesn't –'

'He's not there,' May said, lowering herself on to the wooden bench dimly outlined outside the hut. 'He's gone.' She looked with surprise at the thin trunks of trees glittering in the night. 'Is that the sea?' she asked Balfour, her head down, listening to the sound of waves breaking all about them, seeing her toes lying like pebbles in the grass.

'It's just the t-trees,' he told her, and she looked up and saw the forest moving and a grey smear of light shifting across the tops of the trees like a ridge of mountains. 'You went on about a moon,' she accused the white-shirted Lionel. 'Where is it now?'

'It's gone down behind the hill, sweetheart.' He laughed jovially and spread his cold fingers across her neck, digging his thumb into the hollow behind her ear.

May was so cold sitting out here in this damn countryside, feeling her bones bitten into by the coldness. Ice was forming on her eyeballs. She would die of the cold. 'I want to go home,' she said with difficulty, clamping her jaws together to stop her teeth from breaking against each other. And louder, more

84

firmly, anger giving her warmth, 'I can't stand the bloody place, Lionel, I can't.'

'Hush, hush, sweetheart,' he said, rubbing at her back with his knuckles. 'You'll soon be in beddy-byes.'

George came back along the path with his storm lantern held at shoulder height, his shadow running like a river behind him. The silver birches at the side of the path lost their slenderness. Splotches of brown smeared the fattened trunks. The grass lay flat like hay gone rotten in the rain.

It was only a little warmer inside the hut. George hung the lantern from an iron hook in the ceiling and the wooden walls rolled outwards and back as the lamp twisted above their heads.

'I'll go now,' he said, standing in the doorway, his long face white and his eyes never quite looking at them. Despite his height and the terrible size of his boots he appeared insubstantial. He opened the door and the wind blew at the lantern and shadows disintegrated the quiet pool of his face. He went out of the door, without saying goodnight. May listened for his footsteps, but she couldn't hear anything.

Maybe, thought May, he had simply flown, like some terrible bird to his nest higher up the hillside.

Lionel was fussing about the bedding.

'How many blankets, old man?' he asked Balfour, looking about the room for another doorway. 'Bedroom through there, eh?' he said, nodding his head in the direction of the kitchen, his hands caressing the army-issue blankets of the upper bunk.

'No, there's no b-bedroom. That's the kitchen, L-Lionel.'

'The kitchen.' He looked up incredulously at the discomfited Balfour and then at the double-tiered bunks on either side. 'I say,' he began, smiling broadly, and stopped, not wishing to appear suggestive. It was, he thought, a bit of a lark. A bit not on, of course, but still quite a lark. He hoped his sweetheart would see the funny side. She was sitting hunched and shivering with cold, on the rocker by the black stove.

'Sweetheart,' he called. 'We're all together.'

'I know,' May said, massaging the ends of her toes and noting the cuffs of mud on the sleeves of Lionel's best jacket.

Relieved, Lionel decided it would be more sensible to move one bunk unit to the other end of the hut, near to the kitchen opening – more privacy for the little woman. He began to drag the iron frame across the wooden floor. Balfour helped him. It was the second time that day that they had carried a bed together.

'What are you doing?' May asked. She was damned if she was going to let Lionel sleep on one of those narrow beds with her.

'Just making a little more space,' he panted, his large nose resting on the side of the upper bunk, his ginger moustache sunk in the bedding. He positioned the bedstead sideways across the room, shutting out the kitchen doorway, and draped a blanket from the top bunk to the floor. It would mean less warmth, but it did curtain them off quite successfully. He stepped back to admire his arrangements and smiled at Balfour with satisfaction.

'Very good, old boy ... pretty good, don't you think?'

'Very good,' agreed Balfour, wondering if the little woman would perversely insist on sleeping above, so that it would be the orderly Lionel who would be modestly hidden away behind his curtain, leaving May with her breasts exposed in the moonlight. Shaken, he went to the red curtains and drew them together, though it was black as pitch outside. Better to be sure, he thought, though the moon was not needed to make May visible to him. Imagination alone would fill the occupied hut with light.

He said, 'I'll just take a walk round till you're s-settled, till Mrs' – he stumbled, not knowning what to call her – 'till you're settled.'

'All right, old boy.' Lionel appreciated his thoughtfulness. 'We'll be as quick as we can,' he said. 'Shall I give you a call, old boy?'

But Balfour had already fled into the damp wood.

May knew she must look awful, absolutely awful. Probably blue with the cold and her hair all over the place and her make-up rubbed clean off her face. She would have liked to beautify herself quickly before Balfour returned, but she didn't want to give Lionel the comfort of thinking she was back to normal again. She could hear him on the other side of the bunks, behind that ridiculous blanket, running water in the kitchen. Dear God, did he really expect she would rinse herself in a bucket of ice?

He called, 'You can wash now, sweetheart. It's all ready for you.'

'I don't want to wash, Lionel.'

There was a moment's silence. Only a moment. The resourceful Lionel appeared with a bowl in his hands, manoeuvring himself around the bedstead, slopping water as he came.

'Now, now, little love. Your sweetheart will help you.'

Gently, yet not wasting time, for he was considerate of the walking Balfour, Lionel slipped her sandals free and splashed her feet with water.

'Sweetheart,' he said, 'how warm you are — how we love each other.' He pulled her head down and further disarranged her hair, which reminded her anew of Balfour. If he slept over by the window he would see her face when he awoke. He would surely see her. She couldn't bear anyone to see her when she first awoke. He mustn't sleep by the window. She must make Lionel move the other bunk closer to their own. That way Balfour would be so near he would never dare to look at her, not without branding himself as a Peeping Tom. He would just have to bound out of bed in the morning embarrassed, leaving her in peace to renew her crumpled face.

'Lionel, I'm sorry, but I don't intend sleeping in that bottom bunk with you.' She leaned backwards in the rocking chair and pushed him with her bare foot so that he sat back on his heels.

'Steady on,' he protested, knowing she was about to be

difficult and feeling there wasn't time to cope with it. Couldn't let that poor fellow run about the woods all night. 'What do you want to do?' he asked, defeated.

'You sleep on that bed,' she said, pointing to the bunks at the window.

'That bed?' he repeated, flushing red.

'Not over there. You bring those beds over here and put it beside my bunk.'

'Beside your bunk.' He looked at the window and back again in despair, thinking of Balfour. Didn't she realise what she was suggesting? Didn't she realise the temptation she was throwing in Balfour's path? But of course she didn't. She was so innocent. But it was a bit not on – more than a bit not on. Balfour was bound to get the wrong idea. He said, 'I don't see what you're driving at.' It was one of his expressions. It meant she had offended him.

'I'm not driving at anything. I sleep on the bottom bunk of that bed, and you sleep on the bottom bunk of the other one, and Batman, or whatever his name is, can sleep above you.'

'I see.' His expression was still hurt.

'Well, I'm not bloody well sleeping in that tiny bunk with you and I'm not going to sleep up there on my own with all those animals and things flying around.'

He was touched. How childish she was, not wanting to be alone in the dark. The way she had said 'up there' as if the top bunk were several miles away and swarming with insects. Several of the chaps in his group in the army had been afraid of the dark. He could see her point.

'All right, my darling,' he conceded. 'You just get undressed and get into the bunk and I'll call Balfour.'

'I'm not undressing,' she said. 'It's too cold and you left the suitcases in the other hut.'

He had. It had been foolish of him not to remember. He stood up and took the bowl of water back into the kitchen. Perhaps it was just as well he had been so careless. She could have been warmer and in one of her moods and determined to annoy him. She might have chosen to flaunt herself before Balfour. There had been occasions in the past, one or two, parties and things, when he felt she deliberately sat down with too much leg showing. Nothing very bad, she was too innocent for that, but she did lay herself open to abuse. She just hadn't the experience to know how dangerous her behaviour could be. He constantly had to be on guard to protect her. And himself. She would never know the torment it was for him to see other men looking at her with lust. It filled him with anguish, it unmanned him, he screamed inside himself. He had told her once what he would do if he caught any man messing about with her. He would kill.

'Would you really?' she had asked, her innocent eyes round with fear. 'Would you really kill him, Lionel?'

'Yes, I would.'

'And me, Lionel, what about me?' How frightened her eyes had been.

'I would use karate on you, my sweetheart.'

'Karate?' Her pink mouth opened. Her hands flew upwards.

'A quick blow with the edge of my hand at the pit of your stomach – just there on either side – one-two, and your womanhood would fall to the ground.' How childishly amused she had been, how she had laughed, showing the curved row of white teeth and the pale pink of her moist gums. Everything he said caused her to laugh, she was so innocent.

Tenderly he led her to the curtained bed and removed the coat from about her shoulders, taking his jacket with equal tenderness to the rocking chair, moulding it above the curved back. The bedraggled sleeves brushed the floor.

When he returned to the bed May was under the blankets with her face turned towards the kitchen. He stroked her yellow hair, black in the lamplight, and went to call Balfour.

They dragged the second bunk beside the first and they washed in the dark kitchen, the two men, with the little woman who was so afraid of the dark lying there breathing

89

softly behind their backs. Balfour just knew she wasn't asleep. She was spread out there with her blue eyes wide open, laughing silently at their absurd preparations for the night. What a noise Lionel made swilling water round his mouth. He had left his toothbrush in the other hut, he said. May was sleeping in her clothes because her nightdress was in the suitcase. He hoped Balfour wasn't too inconvenienced by the sleeping arrangements. He came closer in the darkness and whispered sincerely, 'My hands are tied, old boy', and for a second Balfour took him literally, and stood there helplessly, feeling the captive man's breath on his cheek. Hastily he said he understood and felt for the cold water tap with his invisible fingers. Was Lionel stripping himself naked? Would he move, huge flanks scarred with bullets, into the lantern light? Balfour stayed in the corner of the kitchen, endlessly turning his hands in water so cold that it burnt him.

'Will you see to the lamp, old boy?' Lionel asked finally. Half way down him a pair of little shorts caught a shaft of light.

Balfour waited till he felt Lionel must have come to rest. He threw the water noisily down the sink and cleared his throat. He hung his pullover and his trousers on the nail above the back door and stood in his bootless feet trying to smell himself, wondering if he should remove his socks or not. He decided not. He crept, partly naked, and defenceless with cold, into the main room, dragging a chair to the centre of the hut, stepping on it with body curled away from the recumbent May, turning down the wick of the lamp, and fading with it into blackness. He padded to the bunks and placed his foot on the lower bed. He thought maybe Lionel would give his merry laugh, but there was absolute silence in the Arctic night.

Hauling himself aloft, Balfour squirmed into his blankets and pushed his head under the clothes for warmth. He could hear his own breathing and his own heart beating and the sound made by the straw mattress he lay on, as he moved. Nothing stayed in his head. He tried to visualise the horizontal May, with her malicious eyes covered by the flannel sheets

90

and her busty breasts bunched high in her gingham blouse. But he was almost asleep. Hours seemed to have passed. He poked his congested face above the bedding and settled his head more comfortably.

'Sweetheart,' whispered Lionel, 'Are you awake ... are you?'

He felt with his large hand for her shoulder and she hissed angrily, 'Go away, Lionel, be quiet.'

'I just want to know if you're quite comfortable, my darling.'

She wouldn't answer. She jerked her head backwards and forwards on the pillow and compressed her lips in the darkness. She daren't turn away from him. It was too black facing in that direction – and besides, that man up there might think she was moving into Lionel's arms. She didn't want him to think she was lying close to anyone, not anyone as awful as Lionel.

'Let me tell you a story, my darling ... only a short one ... Just you lie still and I'll tell you a story.' He was putting his thick fingers under her neck, feeling for the little hollow under her ear, treading the skin as if she were a heavy object he needed to lever upright.

'Go away,' she whispered as loudly as she dared, lifting her head fractionally, so that he hooked his arm about her neck on the instant and she could feel the ginger moustache brushing her cheek.

'Lie quite still, little sweetheart, little Lalla Rookh ...'

She lay pinned beneath his weight, his body half in her bunk and half in his own, his bald head bobbing up and down above her.

'Sssh,' she said weakly, 'sssh.'

Balfour heard the whispers. One moment he was poised on the very brink of sleep and the next he was wide awake, his eyes cold under the timbered roof, his chest constricted.

'Sweetheart,' breathed Lionel. 'Listen to me, sweetheart. This is the story of Lalla Rookh, goddess of the temple. In the eleventh year of the reign of Aurungzebe, Abdalla, King of the

Lesser Bucharian, set out on a pilgrimage to the shrine of the Prophet, and passing into India through the valley of Kashmir rested at Delhi on the way, where he was entertained most lavishly. It was not long before he heard of the beauty of the renowned Lalla Rookh, Priestess of the Temple of Love. She was, he was told, more lovely than Leila, Shirine or Dewilde, or any of the heroines of the songs of Persia and Hindustan. She was small and rounded with breasts as white as snow and nippes as red as the thorns of the rose ...'

May didn't hear the words at all. She was thinking about her mother and father and how long it was since she had last been to see them. She ought to have visited them, she ought to have sent them some money. They were her family. Her mother wouldn't like her to lie in some rotten hut with this strange old man telling her stories in the night. Her mother called her May, or My Daughter, not Sweetheart or Lalla Rookh. Her mother knew who she was ...

' ... When he came at last to the temple and saw Lalla Rookh for the first time he was utterly ravished. She stood on the steps of the golden altar, dressed in a robe of transparent gauze, with the tips of her toenails dyed blood-red and a gold rod in her hands ...'

Balfour, alone in the upper air, was huge and bloated with excitement. Legs, arms, stomach, mind ballooned out into the darkness, leaving only his head pinned to the pillow like some specimen butterfly.

' ... Abdalla bowed low to the beautiful Lalla Rookh and seated himself on a low stool to observe her performance. First the handmaidens, each one with a cornelian of Yemen about her neck, still in their robes of deepest mourning, knelt before Lalla Rookh and licked the soles of her feet. She stood with eyes demurely lowered ...'

May was thinking about the age of her mother. Not an old woman, she wouldn't die for years yet. Even if she never visited her, it was comforting to know she was alive. It made one old if one's mother died, it was the beginning of the end.

Or the end of her beginning ... Wasn't it futile the way one forgot what mothers did? All that loving and kissing and rocking and changing. All those mothers smelling of woollies and bread. Either you were with someone or you weren't, it didn't really matter. Lionel thought he loved her and thought she loved him. It didn't matter. Either the person wasn't right or the time wasn't, or love came out as something else ... Take Lalla Rookh – she didn't really care for Abdalla or he for her. It was just they were all so perfumed in those days and sexy, and it was all right to behave like that in church in those days.

' ... and now the lovely Lalla Rookh was standing before the great Abdalla, naked to his eyes. "Eyes of mine, why do you droop? Golden dreams, are you coming back again ...".'

That was a lovely thing to say, she thought. He always said that at some point in the story. Even if it was the version about Lalla Rookh and the donkey in Port Said. 'Eyes of mine, why do you droop?'

Later on, when Abdalla had ravished her and gone away, there was the other bit, the poetry bit Lionel liked reciting:

'But see – he starts – what heard he then?
That dreadful shout across the glen:
"They come – the Moslems come," he cries,
His proud soul mounting to his eyes ...'

' ... slowly the lovely Lalla Rookh, thrust her abdomen at the mouth of the mighty Abdalla, her mound of Venus against his throat, the perfume of her sex assailing his nostrils ...'

Outside the wind howled like voices singing a sea song. The unlit paraffin lamp quivered imperceptibly above the wooden floor.

' ... naked came I out of the womb of my mother, said Abdalla the King, casting his garment from him and seizing the wanton Lalla Rookh ...'

It shouldn't happen to a d-dog, thought Balfour, grinding his teeth lest he moaned.

6

In the morning when Joseph woke it was raining. He went
through to the kitchen and filled the kettle with water. He had
dressed and walked through the little hut without feelings of
any kind. Now, triggered by the sight of the unwashed cups in
the sink, he became irritated. Someone had spilled grease on
the draining board. There was Monopoly money in a long
streak of water under the utility table and a cup half filled with
discoloured liquid, possibly coffee, with three drowned and
disintegrating cigarette butts. Where was the ashtray he had
found for Dotty last night? He had been wasting his time
expecting her to use the saucer he had placed at her elbow. It
was typical of her whole attitude.

He rubbed his face with his hands as if to erase Dotty's
memory and the disgust she aroused in him, peering into the
looking-glass by the window, liking his brown skin. The
reflection helped to restore him, but not wholly. There was
something somewhere inside him that persisted. Not
unhappiness, not pain. He walked away from the deceptive
mirror and opened the door to look out at the field lying green
under the falling rain. Mist was covering the hills, rolling
down sideways towards the Glen, unfolding the mountain
inch by inch, uncovering the cotton-wool trees on the lower
slopes. Still he remained heavy and unyielding. What *was*
wrong within him?

He stepped out into the field, away from the sleeping Dotty, and walked through the wet grass in his bare feet to the swing he had made for Roland, reaching out for the rope with one hand as if to anchor himself to something, seeking in his mind for a clue. He must list his worries, his problems. But he was too absent-minded. Thoughts slid across his mind and curled to nothingness. Roland ... Dotty ... his bank manager. I must do ... If I write a cheque post-dated ... I should tell her to use the ash tray. He saw himself bent over his cheque book, Dotty lying with her face against the pillow, Kidney hanging from the bough of a tree ... Dear Sir, With reference to your letter of ... His toes threaded with grass, he stamped his feet. George had planted two young trees in the corner of the field. Mountain ash, circled by stakes; to protect the hut from the winds, George said. In time. How many years before the trees grew high enough and thick enough to be effective? Fifty perhaps. George was planting for posterity.

Dotty was sitting at the table with her head in her hands. She had felt that if she rose before Joseph and prepared breakfast he would be pleased. She thought when she woke that possibly he had gone for a walk through the woods, and she was disappointed at seeing him standing outside the hut staring at the mountain. It was no use starting the breakfast, he would only tell her she was doing it inefficiently.

'My, my,' said Joseph. 'Couldn't you sleep?' He was pushing books aside on the shelves of the little bookcase. A pen and a bottle of aspirins fell to the floor. 'Where's the notepaper?' he asked.

'Top shelf,' she said without looking up.

'I had the most extraordinary dream,' he told her, coming to the table with the writing pad in his hand.

'Oh yes.' She didn't know why he persisted in being so interested in his dreams. It didn't seem to help him much to know what they meant. Sometimes she felt it would be more valuable to him if he wrote down what he did in his waking hours.

'A pen,' he said. 'Where's the pen, Dotty?'

'You knocked it on the floor.'

'Did I? You don't have to sound so critical. I merely asked where it was.' He began trying to put down his dream on paper. 'Listen to this, Dot-Dot ... I was in bed with my father. It was very dark and he was just lying there ... It was at home ... In Wales, I mean, and my father said, "I've got an attack coming." I said, "What shall I do?" and then –'

He looked up hastily and Dotty said, 'I'm listening. Go on. I'm just going for my tobacco ... Go on ... You said, "What shall I do?".' She searched for her tobacco on a chair and failed to find it. Straightening up, she saw the field outside, framed by the window, like a picture someone had hung on a wall.

'What attacks were they?'

But Joseph wouldn't answer her. He sat at the table and shut her out, keeping his eyes lowered, pushing the little plastic pen about.

She put the kettle on and went out of the hut in her nightgown. The wood spread over her like a great arched umbrella. Underneath the green spokes she was perfectly dry. There was the red tree Roland had talked about. She crossed to the door of the Barn and went in. Roland was sitting up in bed, his hands clutching the blankets.

'Hallo,' she said, looking for Kidney in the other bed and finding him, curled sideways with his hair spread across the pillow.

'I've been bitten by something,' Roland said, holding up one thin arm for inspection. 'Look ... it's fleas or bugs.'

'Surely not.' She bent closer and looked at the two red marks on the delicate white forearm. 'Not fleas, Roland, they can't be.'

'Why not?' He scratched himself hard and looked down with approval at the swollen skin.

'Well, you only get fleas in dirty places. This isn't dirty. We're in the country with all the flowers and things.' She

96

found her flesh beginning to itch and rubbed at her neck worriedly.

'It *is* dirty in the country,' Roland asserted. Some of the sting had gone out of his arm. 'Anyway,' he said, 'we had fleas at home and Mummy got the Health Man and it's not dirt that makes fleas.'

She was shocked. 'Did you have fleas at home?'

'Fleas can be in houses for ever and ever. A flea's egg can live for a hundred years and then you make everywhere nice and warm and the flea comes out, hundreds of years old but all new. It's thirty shillings a room for bugs and ten shillings for fleas, and it's free for mice and rats.'

'Is it?' she said, interested and repelled.

'When the Health Man came, Mummy and I had to go to the park for a walk and he threw bombs in all the rooms. The smoke stuff killed all the fleas by the time we came home for tea.'

'That's good,' said Dotty. Kidney rolled over on to his back and thrust his feet hard down the bed. He made a sound between a snore and a cough.

'Good morning, Kidney,' Dotty said, but he went on sleeping.

'The man couldn't kill all the fleas,' said the obsessed Roland. 'Mummy didn't have enough ten shillings for the bathroom or the hall. I expect they'll come back. When we had tea he read the Bible to us.' He knelt in the bed and pressed his nose to the window. 'Is it cold?' he asked.

'No,' Dotty said, only a little chill in her white nightgown hemmed with mud.

'I don't suppose my Dad will take me up the mountain.' The little boy didn't look at her for a denial. He kept his eyes fixed on the square of grey sky and rubbed at his bitten arm.

'Did you sleep well?' Dotty wanted to know, feeling the bed with her hand to assess its comfort.

'All right.' Roland fell backwards on to her lap and twisted his arms about her neck. He liked being with Dotty. The time

97

before when he had been to stay with Joseph there had been a pretty girl with a long plait down her back. He'd liked being with her too. He didn't know there would be a girl in the woods with Daddy. When Daddy came in the car to fetch him at Mummy's there had only been Kidney. Daddy had found Dotty just round the corner without any suitcase or even a coat. Dotty's hair was nice. It looked like the beige curtains hung in his room at home.

'Carry me, carry me,' he demanded, burying his face in the familiar curtains. 'Ooooh,' he squealed, as they left the trees and the rain fell on to his neck. Dotty held him tightly in her arms for the benefit of Joseph and her own image, but Joseph was bent over the table still wrestling with his dream.

'Hallo, boy,' he said, not looking up. 'Kettle's boiling, Dotty,' he added, jerking his head in the direction of the cooker.

'Did you sleep all right?' she heard him ask Roland. 'Kidney didn't disturb you, did he?'

'He lets off all night.'

'Roland knows an awful lot about fleas,' Dotty said, bringing them cups of tea and a saucer for the fussy Joseph. 'He says he's been bitten by some.'

'I have, I have.' Eagerly the child rolled back his pyjama sleeve and peered at his arm. 'They were there,' he cried, disappointed, tearing at the smooth skin with his nails, trying to bring back the swellings.

'Nonsense,' Joseph said. 'I can't see anything.' He flipped the cover of the writing pad over the notes he had made and lifted Roland on to his knee.

'He did have some marks,' Dotty confirmed, but the two of them were whispering together, not aware of her at all.

She went once more out of the hut. Holding the cup of tea in her hands for warmth, she sat down on the decaying wooden step at the door. What did one do in the country, she wondered? Maybe they should go for long walks or have picnics. They might just as well be back in the flat off the

98

Finchley Road – her making the tea and Kidney fast asleep and Joseph scribbling away at his dreams. It was safer at home. The constricted space forced Joseph to come close to hurt her. Here she could lose him.

She leaned her head against the wet doorpost and yawned.

As soon as he awoke, Balfour left the hut, neither pausing to wash nor cook himself breakfast. The recollections of the night before followed him out into the wood. He was damp with recollection, saturated. He walked limply under the rain-filled trees towards the Big House. He found it difficult to separate what had happened from what he imagined. He longed to confide in someone. George was on the plateau of the house, holding a branch across a three-legged stool, sawing the wood into logs of equal length.

'C-could I make a cup of tea?' Balfour asked. 'I didn't want to make too much noise in the hut like.'

George said, 'I thought Joseph could light the stove in Hut 4.' He looked out across the valley.

'Good idea,' said Balfour, sitting down on the slate slabs.

'The kettle's boiling, I expect,' George told him. 'If you call me when it's ready I'll join you.' He gazed at Balfour a moment before poising the sharp teeth of the saw above the waiting branch.

Balfour made the tea in Mrs MacFarley's earthenware teapot and waited on the tidy bed for the mixture to brew. He wanted to talk to George and he knew there wasn't much point. It wasn't as if he and George could have a good old giggle together. Hardly likely.

'George,' he shouted. 'George – tea up.'

George entered the door, blocking out the light, his shapeless hat dripping water.

'It was a bit rum last night,' blurted Balfour. 'Lionel p-put the bunks together and she was in the lower bunk and he in the other, and I was on top like, and he told her stories half the night.'

99

George looked as if he understood. He sat down and regarded Balfour gravely for several seconds. 'Did you sing?' he asked, his eyes sliding away from the face below him, studying the map above Balfour's head.

'No,' said Balfour.

'I thought I heard singing last night from the hut ... I thought I did ... I wanted to come back and join you, but I felt I should wait till I was included ...'

'We weren't singing,' protested Balfour. 'Nobody sang a note. He just told her stories all night – all about someone called Larry O'Rourke.'

'Is he Irish?' George enquired. 'The Irish are very fond of singing.'

'They weren't stories really,' Balfour floundered. 'I mean I couldn't hear them properly. They were private like ... all about this fella O'Rourke and a t-temple somewhere.' He closed his mouth at the memory.

'He was in the East,' George said. 'He was in Palestine.'

Bloody hell, thought Balfour, angrily jabbing at his inflamed neck. He wondered whether Lionel was awake now, already muttering his tales into the ear of the little woman. What a way to greet the day, like 'Lift up Your Hearts ...' with a kick in it.

George said, 'You could help me carry the logs over to the hut later if you have a moment.' He stood up, shifting his head a little from side to side, looking down at Balfour and away again. He went out of the hut and on to the rain-drenched plateau. He wasn't at ease about Balfour – the drinking of the first evening, the rhyme about the Jew in a cave of last night. Like the sudden outbreak of fire in the scrub, nothing was entirely accidental nor entirely planned. Chaos could escalate to such a point that what preceded it achieved a degree of order. He didn't wish the chaotic Balfour to become less ordered. No man could foresee with accuracy the type of feeling generated by another. Evil lay beyond the Glen – the emotion of evil – waiting to devour the trees and the valley, waiting to burst into flame. Soon he would be able to discuss such problems with Joseph. They wouldn't of course allude to evil by its name, they would talk about faulty materials and bad planning and cheap design. He didn't delude himself that Joseph would be of much help to him. He had too many things adhering to his life that hindered – marriage and women friends and a responsible job. He must wait a few days until the peace of the Glen had smoothed out the creased Joseph.

Balfour made a clumsy job of securing the wood into a bundle that could be carried. He was hampered by the fact that he wished to get away across the stream before Lionel and May awakened and sought him out. The thought of facing them with only the detached George for protection filled him with anxiety.

'That's no use,' George told him. Methodically, he placed the logs in correct lengths on the plateau, slipping a leather belt underneath the roll and drawing the thong tight.

Balfour looked in the direction of Hut 2 and imagined he saw the curtains move across the window. Loaded correctly, he was set on the down path to the stream. George turned about from time to time to comment on the vista before the Big House. 'We should lop a few more trees,' he said. 'From certain angles the plateau is quite obscured.'

Balfour could smell the bacon frying even as they climbed the slope above the bridge. Roland was being pushed on the swing by Dotty, still in her nightdress. She looked, he thought, a funny girl, standing there in the damp grass with her large feet sticking out from beneath the bedraggled hem of her gown. The child and the girl looked at George in his odd hat and Balfour with his pile of logs, but they didn't speak. Balfour thought they were all a bit daft, all of them – no one saying a word of greeting, not even a bit of a smile. Gloomily he went to the door of the hut and waited for George to open it for him.

'What's all this about?' Joseph asked of George authoritatively, pointing at the wood with a long knife in his

101

hand, ignoring the beast of burden beneath it. He hadn't really noticed the stove alongside the settee. He kicked at its brick base with his shoe and wanted to know if it worked. He wanted to know if it smoked much, if they could use it for cooking. He sounded angry and suspicious, as if George were trying to sell him something. Balfour let the logs fall on to the settee and went to wash his hands at the sink. The bacon was spitting in the pan. On the floor by the calor gas container was the tartan holdall of groceries that Balfour had carried for Lionel.

Dotty came in and looked anxiously at the frying pan on the cooker. 'That's not our food, Joseph,' she said.

'Quite right, Dotty.' He brought out a bag of sugar and placed in on the table. 'Call Roland, will you.'

Roland had bacon and some slices of bread dipped in fat. Joseph asked Dotty if she wanted bacon too, but she suspected it was Lionel and May's and refused, saying she wasn't hungry. It was untrue. She was huge and vicious with hunger, but she sat there with a mug of tea in her hand and refrained from eating even a piece of bread. 'Don't you think,' she said finally, 'that you ought to give Kidney something to eat?'

'No, I don't,' Joseph told her. 'He's far too fat.' He studied the palm of his hand, holding it up to the light as if gazing at a rare stamp.

I shall never kiss you again, she thought spitefully, and then sorrowfully, I shall never kiss you again. When the week was up she would go to her parents' home and write him a letter asking him to send all her things to her. That wasn't really a good idea – she might never see her books or clothes again, he was so bad about that sort of thing.

As if reading her thoughts, as if the possibility of her leaving him made him generous, he said, 'Go on, Dot-Dot, have some of Lionel's bacon.'

'Joseph's had another of his dreams,' she told George. 'He writes them all down.'

'I never dream,' said George.

102

'Oh, but you do,' cried Joseph. 'All the time. You just don't remember them. The mind,' he explained, 'is less inhibited when we sleep. We can be our true selves then – given vent to all kinds of repressed desires, act out our fantasies, behave without the restraints imposed by society.'

'Some people,' Dotty said, 'are like that when they're awake.' She got up and went in search of her tobacco.

Balfour was fidgeting on his chair, fearing any moment the arrival of Lionel and May. He chatted with Roland about his red boat, telling him it was a lovely boat, standing up and taking it to the window to admire it.

'Oh God,' Dotty moaned distractedly. She went through the aperture into the cubicle and Balfour followed, squeezing past her in the constricted space, stepping into the second room with the truckle bed.

'What are you doing?' she asked.

'Lionel,' he mouthed, pointing ridiculously with one frantic finger at the wall. 'Out there.' He fumbled with the bolt of the back door and held it close with his hand.

'What's the matter?' she asked, coming close, her eyes shining with curiosity.

'Sssh,' he warned.

Outside Lionel shouted cheerfully, 'Ahoy there.' There was the sound of footsteps at the door. The wooden wall of the cubicle vibrated as he entered.

'What is it?' whispered Dotty.

Anguished, Balfour shook his head and stepped into the field, standing there in the rain, his head tilted to catch the sound of Lionel's voice.

'What is it?' Dotty persisted, stepping outside the hut and hanging on to his arm.

'I just don't want to see Lionel.'

'Why not? What happened?' She shook him. 'Go on, tell me.' She pushed her washed-out face close to his.

'He told stories all night.' He swung his head round, hearing Lionel move inside the hut, and suddenly felt foolish.

Dotty was looking at him, less eagerly, but still with that curious degree of elation on her features.

'What do you mean, he told her stories? What kind of stories?'

'Well, funny ones – ones I shouldn't think he wanted me to hear. But I did hear like. Blinking rum stories,' he added bleakly, detesting the way he spoke, wondering why at work he was considered a bit of a talker, in spite of his stammer, not understanding why he should find it difficult to express himself to this lot – Joseph and Dotty and the rest of them.

'Rum?' said Dotty. 'Do you mean dirty?'

That was tricky, thought Balfour. He didn't know if they were dirty – not in artistic circles, that is – though somehow Lionel didn't seem in the least like Joseph or George. More like himself – and he'd thought they were dirty all right. 'I don't know about that,' he said, feeling hungry and not at all sure. He couldn't think why he was making such a fuss.

'Poor Balfour,' she said and reached up and touched his cheek with the back of her hand. 'Poor Balfour. Don't you worry, boyo.' She sounded genuinely concerned, amused and yet anxious for him. 'They're all a bit rum, aren't they?' She was the conspirator again.

'A bit,' he admitted.

'They are, aren't they? I mean, they really are, don't you think? I mean, look at Joseph, going all moody and never being polite to anyone, and Lionel going on about the army, and May saying she hates him. They're all barmy.'

'I don't know,' he said, looking at his feet, not wanting to commit himself.

'Well, you don't feel comfortable, do you? I mean, it's obvious. You didn't stutter at all when we first came. Not that I noticed. I bet you're like you were the other night when you'd had a few drinks – I mean, like that all the time normally.'

'I've always had a s-stutter,' Balfour said, wanting to be off through the trees. He knew it wasn't the others that were odd, but himself who was at fault. He couldn't get his bearings. If he'd heard some bloke at the factory telling a smutty yarn he'd have laughed like hell. The dirtier the better. He wouldn't be like he was now – sort of morally indignant and feeling like he was shocked. Old Lionel probably had his reasons for getting his kicks out of telling her stories. The little woman was a man-eater. He couldn't make a judgment on Joseph yet. Old George he knew about – he'd got used to not being able to talk to him. There was something wrong within himself, something he could sense but not explain.

Roland had been told to go looking for larch twigs for the fire they were going to have in that stove thing by the sofa. May said it was too cold to live, so they were going to light a fire later on to keep her alive. He knew they weren't going up the mountain today on account of the wet, though it wasn't raining any more – even the trees had stopped dripping. The grass was untidy. Over the hedge there was a field full of mauve thistle tops that stuck in his feet, painful as anything, and he'd seen a cow yesterday with long white legs galloping like a horse through all those prickles, with its tail held straight out in the air and Joseph said a horsefly was probably bothering it. Most of the leaves on the trees by the barn had been eaten by something – lots of little holes bitten in the leaves, showing spots of sky, as if someone had spattered the trees with white paint, all tatty-looking. Moths or something. The ferns by the bushes hadn't been bitten – they smelt too strong – nor the nettles. There wasn't a dock leaf in sight. His teacher at school had told him that wherever God put a stinging nettle he put a dock leaf next to it. Children, she had said, run to the lowly dock leaf and rub its juice over the sting of the stinging nettle. It wasn't the truth and he would tell her. There were thousands of nettles and not a single dock leaf. He had looked.

He wanted to go up the mountain because it looked safe out there: nothing dangerous on it, no wire netting like under the barn step, through which the wasps went, buzzing pale green and angry. He supposed it wasn't much use telling Joseph it had stopped raining. Joseph didn't want to take him up the mountain. They were all talking in there about that war, and bombs dropping on things, and about Germany. It sounded dangerous in there too. Besides, Joseph was going vista-clearing with George, and he had seemed so pleased about it – jumping up and swinging his arms as if he were holding an axe, and Lionel laughing at him – that it wouldn't be kind to mention the mountain again. Lionel said 'vista' came from the Italian, and George said they weren't going to chop any trees down, only lop off a few branches. 'Vista' sounded sad, like saying goodbye. They said he could go for the milk tonight, on his own, to the farm. That was to make up for not going vista-clearing or up the mountain or with Dotty and Balfour to the village to spend his two-shilling piece. He couldn't go to the village with them because they were walking and they said it was too far for him to walk. There wasn't any food left to eat, only Ribena and red peppers.

He didn't have to get those twigs for the fire. No one really expected him to go for them – it was just to make him feel big and busy while they finished their chat about the war. It was only when he was with Joseph that he wanted to be big. When he was with Joseph it was always 'Lift that, you're a big boy now', or 'Climb that tree, Roland ... Higher ... you're big enough', as if it showed he wasn't big enough at all. Not like Kidney. If he could grow as big as Kidney, Joseph and he might do exercises in the morning on the tree and climb the mountain, and do vista-clearing all the time.

Dotty had said she'd bring him back a notebook from the village for him to write in. He would write a story like Joseph. It would be a dream story. Joseph had asked him if he had ever had a dream. He was starting to tell him, only Lionel and May came in and Dotty said she was sorry Joseph had eaten all their bacon and used their sugar.

106

He heard the door of the barn creak and he looked round the side of the hut and saw Kidney.

'What are you looking at, please?' asked Roland joining him.

'I'm looking,' said Kidney, screwing his face up till his eyes almost disappeared.

'What are you looking at?'

'A silver birch,' Kidney said.

Roland stared too. He could see Kidney's shoes all scruffy with dried mud, and a rock lying beneath the bushes, and he could see the tree. The birch was wet, its bark gleaming after the rain, and there were four ants joined like a thread of cotton clinging to its trunk. Ants in the grass were hardworking and stupid. They only itched. Those ants on the tree were lazy and clever. They would sting like pins going in. He moved quite close, fascinated and afraid.

'Those?' he asked.

'Yes.'

'What are they doing?'

Kidney said he didn't know. He swung his head sorrowfully and told Roland he was going for his breakfast. 'I'm hungry and I want my pills.'

'The ones in the bottle?'

'I need my breakfast.'

'You shouldn't eat those pills in the bottle. You should swing on trees.' Kidney was walking away and Roland shouted, 'There's no food left and they're all talking about that war.' He watched the hungry Kidney push open the door and disappear with lowered head.

The war talk went on for a long time.

May wouldn't speak to Lionel. She was obviously huffy. She shielded her face with one hand and played with her spoon in the unappetising mess of her shredded wheat. She felt exhausted and hideous, with all her make-up on wrong. The mirror was too small, and when she had done her eyebrows Joseph had made some remark about her warpaint and they had all watched her. She was sure she had swollen in the night; she felt blown out like some balloon. It was water retention or something horrible like that. She couldn't think how Dotty could walk around in that cotton sack in this weather. Lionel had told her to put on another sweater if she wasn't warm enough, but she was damned if she was going to add to her already large proportions. The hairdresser in the King's Road had sworn her set would last a week – four or five days at the least – and already it was out. It was dreadful. Those army blankets had given her some kind of skin allergy too, she was convinced of it. She could feel the little broken veins in her cheeks and there was a rough patch on her neck. Lionel of course looked much the same as usual, the same as he ever did. He'd pushed his head into that tin bowl of cold water and come up all red and spluttering. The way he scrubbed his face with the towel it was a wonder he didn't wear his skin through to the bone. He'd changed into a checked shirt with a silly green cravat at the throat, with that coin of his hidden behind it and his elderly heart going boom-boom-boom on the other side. She was grateful it wasn't summery enough for his appalling shorts, the khaki ones that came below his knees. It was such a small hut with all these people in it. There wasn't room to breathe and it was so dark with the door shut, as if they were in a ship's cabin with the spray splashing up against the porthole. There was more space further in, towards that chintz sofa – which was an odd piece of furniture to find in this place – but it was warmer nearer the cooker. There was something large and grey standing near the wall, shaped like an unexploded bomb with a metal knob on it. She hoped it wouldn't blow up. Lionel was going on about Churchill being a great man, talking about him as if he'd met him, saying he spoke to him at Malta once. He always pretended that. He never had met him.

108

'Great man, a great man of history. I had the honour once of meeting him ...'

Balfour said, 'I watched the funeral on telly. It was sad.'

'Who are we talking about?' asked Joseph, looking round with a puzzled expression.

'Lionel met Winston Churchill, and Balfour saw him on telly,' Dotty said, miserable without her tobacco. She knew Joseph had heard Lionel, he was just being awkward.

'He had a remarkable ability,' Lionel was saying, 'to get close to the ordinary man.'

May said, 'I couldn't bear that awful siren-suit he wore. What did he have to wear that dreadful thing for?'

'Ah, my sweetheart, how little you understand. The man, Churchill, the historical figure, was behind his siren suit. In his case, clothes could hardly matter.'

Clothes do matter, thought May, licking away the grains of sugar folded in the corners of her mouth. If she had the money she would buy a coat the same colour as the shredded wheat, with Italian seams at the waist. With it she'd wear a boy's shirt with buttoned-down collar and cream stockings and toffee patent shoes, and beige nail varnish and lip salve, and just a touch of white shadow above her eyes, on the corner of the lids. It was typical of Lionel not to know that clothes mattered. He'd gone on long enough deploring the loss of the Empire or something, and he couldn't see just how British-mad everyone was now, what with clothes and pop songs and the King's Road on a Saturday morning. Everyone she knew was dreadfully patriotic, and especially if you came from Liverpool. She had told Lionel they ought to buy a Union Jack to hang over their bed. Lionel had just laughed and called her a funny little thing. He didn't believe her when she told him that all the best people, even the Armstrong Jones's possibly, pinned Union Jacks up all over the place. It was the thing. You could get boxes of matches with the flag on, and tea-towels and handkerchiefs and coffee mugs, a shirt if you went

109

to Carnaby Street – anything if you wanted it. And it really had something to do with being glad you were English – as though you knew everything was going decadent and awful, and now was the time you could dress up in style and shout you were British-made.

Lionel was now talking about treaties and organisations. 'South American powers,' he said seriously, 'Asiatic powers, European powers, known collectively as the Great Powers.'

'I only know Tyrone Power,' said May.

Joseph laughed.

'Silly child,' said Lionel indulgently, a little annoyed at her interruption but charmed by her gaucherie and the fact that she had at last spoken. It made him feel freer. It allowed him to speak more personally about the war, his war. He started a long rambling account of his experiences in Malta leading up to his meeting with the Great Man. 'When the show first got under way,' he began. 'After Mr Shickelgrueber had shown his hand ...'

May saw that Dotty was gazing at Lionel, not fluttering her eyelashes at him – she wasn't feminine enough for that – but eyeing him all right. She's so drab, thought May; she's no idea how to exploit her sex. All those ghastly boy's dungarees and sneakers on her feet – size nine, by the look of them. She hadn't been born till the war was over. Fancy that – not even a war baby. Where was that place, she wondered, with the injured soldiers everywhere? They had lived there for a year during the war, after her father had been sent overseas. Southport, was it? The place with the fairy lights in the trees. The soldiers were all dressed in bright bright blue, some on crutches and some without an arm, and a terrible man with a burnt face, candle-pink, and a strip of waxy flesh for a nose. It looked comical really – not the burnt man, poor devil, but all of them, hobbling and limping down the street, under those trees with the lights not on because of the war, just the black bulbs stuck up there like fruit spotted with bird droppings. Some of the wounded soldiers pushed each other in

110

wheelchairs. She'd never liked soldiers, never – they reminded her of Father. They always looked so awful when they put on civilian clothes and couldn't hide behind the uniform any more. She had an uncle, though, who had been in some regiment that made him wear a kilt, and he came on leave once and played the piano, with his legs all bare and the tight little pleats flaring out all round the piano stool, sitting there playing 'Silver Threads Among the Gold'.

Lionel was looking at Dotty with wonder and shaking his head from side to side. 'Incredible,' he said, 'I keep forgetting – not even born.'

'She's too young. Aren't you, Dot-Dot?' Joseph said, patting Dotty's hand.

May smiled too, regarding her husband fixedly, positively daring him to dwell on the youthfulness of Dotty. She didn't pretend to be younger than she was. She wasn't as old as her birth certificate said. She couldn't be. It was a cruel mistake.

'I had a cousin who was killed in Germany,' Dotty volunteered. 'He was shot down over Dresden.'

'I'm terribly sorry,' Lionel said. His grief seemed genuine.

'I never knew him,' Dotty explained. 'I've seen photographs, but I never knew him.'

Lionel pushed the dead relation out of his mind. 'Clever lot, those Germans. Good soldiers, especially under Rommel. They're a nation of soldiers – it's the Prussian influence. They have an instinct for it, just as we had an instinct for colonisation. The warring instinct of the German nation.' He paused. His fingers fumbled with the buttons of his shirt. 'I have here,' he said, clutching something inside his shirt, a symbol that may illustrate what I mean. I don't often show it to anyone. I regard it as sacred.'

'What is it?' Dotty was sure he was talking about the coin, the Blakely Moor token piece. She couldn't look at May.

'A coin,' said Lionel, 'an old coin. I took it from around the neck of a German officer in Italy. There was a small nick at the edge and beneath the coin a round hole in his breast.' He

111

allowed them a glimpse of the metal chain, but that was all.

'A dead German, I hope,' Joseph said, not greatly caring, looking at the still-munching Kidney, who had eaten half a loaf of bread. He wondered whether he should give him a pill now.

'Very dead. He was little more than a boy. Same age as myself actually. But make no bones about it, he was dead.'

How awful, thought May, in part believing the story, seeing the lifeless German and a callous Lionel, little more than a boy, snatching the chain from about his neck. He was so persuasive. Sometimes she wondered if Lionel had ever got further than the Isle of Man. He had told her once that his father, the buried William Gosling, cashier of the bank, had given him the coin, and on another occasion that he'd found it on the windowsill of a farmhouse in France – when he was occupying some place or other, when he was winning the war. The last story he'd told her even after she knew it was the Blakely Moor token for one penny only.

Joseph fetched the bottle of pills from under the settee. He kept the container hidden in his palm, not able to make up his mind about the problem of Kidney – medicine versus exercise. He was going to go vista-clearing with George and he wasn't going to have time to see that the youth did press-ups or ran round and round the field. Those half-dozen slices of white starch Kidney had just consumed weren't exactly the best way to start a day. He fretted that he couldn't concentrate on Kidney, couldn't be singleminded enough to be of real help. He fretted that he was again postponing taking Roland up the mountain, though the child seemed to have forgotten the whole idea.

Lionel was still carrying on about the battlefield and the gunfire. His voice was breaking with recollection.

Joseph, putting the bottle of pills high up on the shelf above the sink, said roughly, 'Come on, George, let's get cracking.'

The tall man rose slowly and Balfour quickly joined him. George lowered his head at the doorway, to step down into the grass.

112

When the three men had gone, May said she had left a lipstick in the front pocket of the car and wanted it. She told Lionel to go at once, waving her hand at him imperiously, and he did as he was told, leaving the two women alone with Kidney. May didn't mind him being there. He didn't count. She jumped to her feet and peered into the mirror, giving a small scream of disgust. 'Ugh.'

'Do you want some hot water?' Dotty put the kettle on and lit the calor gas.

'I hate him, I hate him ... It's all his fault.' May fell on her knees and dragged the suitcase from under the table, pulling out several dresses and some sweaters.

'That's super.' Dotty picked up a skirt, held it against her waist. It looked like an apron on her.

'Well, I can't wear it ... Look at the creases in it.' May snatched it away and bundled it into her case. She sat back on her heels and buried her head in her hands.

'Oh come on, love. It's not as bad as that.'

Kidney was looking earnestly at the writing pad abandoned by Joseph among the dishes. He turned its pages and began to draw something.

When the water was hot Dotty poured it into the bowl for May and found the soap. The woman was so helpless in many ways, she felt compelled to do things for her. May washed her hands and placed her damp fingertips against her face as if the water might do her an injury. 'It's all stinging,' she complained. 'It's those bloody army blankets.'

'What happened last night with Balfour and you?'

'Me and Balfour?'

'He seemed a bit upset. He said Lionel told a dirty story.'

'My God.' May hid her ravaged face behind the towel and turned to the mirror. 'Did he hear?' she asked. 'What did he say?'

'He just said Lionel told you a story.'

'He tells me stories every night ... I don't listen any more ... they're always the same.'

'What are they about?'

113

'Lalla Rookh and some temple.'

Dotty giggled.

'When he first told me them,' – May was spilling the contents of her handbag on to the draining board, fumbling for her foundation cream, unscrewing the gold top on the black tube – 'it was a bit of a shock, I can tell you, but I've got used to it now.' She wasn't going to tell Dotty that Lionel never made love to her, never actually had intercourse. Dotty would probably tell everybody. She said, 'If he can't make love to me, he tells me stories.' She caught sight of Kidney's face in the mirror, his blue eyes fixed on her. 'Is he listening?' she asked, turning round to look at him.

'Shouldn't think so.' Dotty was reminded of the farewell letter she was going to write Joseph, telling him everything in her mind, everything. 'Joseph won't touch me,' she said, searching on the shelves in the inner room for her writing paper. 'He says I revolt him.'

'Really?' May tried to express sympathy and incredulity, but she was too absorbed in her make-up, barely listening to the girl.

'I'm going to write him a long letter,' Dotty said, sitting down on the settee.

'Oh yes.' May's mouth stretched wide as she applied colour to her lips. There were freckles, gold-coloured, on the bridge of her tilted nose.

Dotty wrote:

'Joseph: I don't suppose you will take much notice of this, because I have done this so often, written I mean, threatening to go away and in the end not going ...'

It was true. She wrote him so many letters but she never went.

'But this time I do mean it. It's all to do with me being so awful and people like this girl you've got at the college not being awful. I mean, if I wasn't awful you wouldn't need to

114

go to someone else so quickly. Anyway, I don't see much point in me hanging around just irritating you with my ciggies and my nose, because your wife did that – always around, I mean – and it didn't get her very far, did it?'

May said, 'Why doesn't Joseph play with Roland? He's a sweet little boy. Just look at him.'
Dotty looked up and asked what he was doing.
'He's on the swing, just swinging up and down. He's bored.'
'Oh, he's all right. He adores Joseph.'
She wrote:

'I know it's none of my business and less so now, but you have to be careful of Roland, you have to give him more time. It's all right with me or Kidney or women, but it's different for Roland. You have to see that. Once when I was little ...'

She stopped. She had told Joseph that anecdote before, several times in fact. She re-read the words written and wished she had some cigarettes. Or something to drink. Without tobacco she couldn't possibly tell Joseph what she thought of him. She couldn't tell him she hoped he would rot and end up without friends, only a host of women to whom he paid out conscience money. Neither could she describe in detail her own ugliness or unworthiness – the concentration wasn't there, she just wanted a cigarette. She sat looking at May, who was puffing up her hair with one hand, standing at the sink with her cosmetics in a row on the narrow windowsill.
'My God,' May said, 'here comes the galloping major.'
Lionel entered the hut, carrying Roland on his back. He said he hadn't been able to spot her lipstick, not in the compartment, nor on the back seat, or in the boot, or anywhere.
'Hallow, luv,' Dotty said, and Roland came to the sofa and fell on to it beside her, leaning his head against her shoulder. 'Are you a bit bored? Don't you know what to do with yourself?'

115

'I'm all right. What are you writing?'

'A sort of letter.'

'I'm just going to spend a penny,' Lionel told them, frankly, running out of the hut with his cravat slightly dishevelled.

May said 'Christ!' and came to Roland, her hand rummaging in the depths of her handbag. 'Here,' she said. 'Would you like to play with this?' It was her lighter.

'No thanks.' He got up and stood at the table, pushing the dishes about to disturb the placid Kidney, watching him drawing his flowers.

'Would you like to write to Mummy and I'll post it?' Dotty asked, tearing free a page of her writing paper in expectation.

'No.' The little boy attempted to smile. Dotty had to go to him then, falling on her knees beside him, pushing his face into her neck, feeling his lips quivering against her throat. 'What's wrong, little boy? What's wrong, little love?'

He couldn't speak. He wanted his mother.

'You want Daddy, don't you? Poor little love.' Her voice was angry all at once. She stood up and sat at the table, lifting him with her, placing him on her lap. She looked down fiercely into his desolate face and wiped a tear away with the tip of her finger.

May stood uncertainly with the lighter in her hand. Dotty was so emotional with the child, she was as bad as Lionel. The boy had been perfectly all right, bored perhaps but not miserable. Dotty didn't seem to realise that Roland was like his mother. The mother had terribly wistful eyes, really terribly mournful and bereft, and she was as strong as a man and fat as hell.

After a moment Lionel returned and sat down at the table. He and Roland began a game of noughts and crosses.

116

7

The afternoon was warm and dry. Dotty was practically silent
the whole way to the village, striding along between the
hedgerows with her shoulders hunched and the shopping bag
in her hand. She told Balfour she'd be all right when she got
her ciggies.

The village, to her surprise, turned out to be a fair-sized
market town with a Tesco stores and a Midland Bank. She
purchased at once a packet of Woodbines and said she must
have a cup of tea and a sausage roll. They sat in a cream-tiled
café and she lit her cigarette and closed her eyes. He was
embarrassed by the sight of a tear rolling out from under her
closed lids. 'You've no idea,' she told him, 'how hungry I get.
Honest to God, I get that hungry I could scream.' She ate and
smoked at the same time and colour came into her cheeks.

'It's funny,' she explained, 'me being hungry all the time,
because I don't really enjoy food and I never put on weight. I
wouldn't know one sausage roll from another. Joseph says my
hunger means something else ... But then everything means
something else, doesn't it?'

'I suppose so.'

'Why do you stutter now?' she asked him suddenly. 'You
didn't at first, when we got here ... I didn't notice, anyway.'

He felt awkward and looked down at the table. 'It comes
and goes,' he mumbled.

'I didn't mean ...' She was afraid she had offended him.

117

'I did have a very bad stutter when I was a child,' he confessed. 'B-but Mr and Mrs MacFarley cured me, m-more or less. It gets bad w-when –' he broke off, not really knowing when it got bad.

She made a list of shopping they could do separately to save time.

'Are we in a h-hurry?' asked Balfour, gulping his tea and looking at the clock on the wall. It was a quarter to four.

'No,' there's no hurry, I suppose ... It's just that there's nothing for Roland's supper and we need candles before it gets dark.'

'There's gallons of paraffin in the store shed,' Balfour observed, but she brushed that aside.

'I don't like taking other people's things,' she cried, hunched over her empty plate, licking her fingers and stubbing them against the dish, bringing orange flakes of pastry to her mouth. 'It's so awful sponging on people all the time.'

He felt ill at ease, self-conscious at being seen with her in her denim outfit. The waitress behind the glossy tea urn was staring relentlessly.

'We'll get started then,' he said, jerking his head at the woman at the counter and feeling in his pocket for money.

She wouldn't let him pay for her. 'Honest to God, I can't let you pay for my sausage roll,' she told him, grimacing as she dug down into the back pocket of her trousers.

His face burning, he walked along the street. Down a side turning were stalls with vegetables and fruit. There was cheap jewellery and cheap glass, and further along a rail of second-hand clothing. He stopped on the corner and she caught hold of his arm with her spiky fingers and asked, 'Are you angry with me, love? You are, I know you are.' She wrung her hands in anguish and passersby turned curiously to look at them.

'I don't know what you mean,' he said, walking down the side street with the shopping list crumpled in his hand.

In silence she regarded the trays of plastic brooches and

118

metal rings. He hung his head beside her. 'You're just like Joseph,' she accused him. 'I irritate you, don't I?'

'Please,' he begged, out of his depth and able neither to proceed nor stand still.

It was then that she saw the clothes. 'Look,' she cried, running towards the stall, pushing aside the coats and dresses, the curtains of hair enveloping her face and her arms flying out as she separated the hanging garments, 'Aren't they smashing. Look at this ... and this ...' Her face when she turned to Balfour was bright with happiness.

'It might suit you,' he said, looking at the man's anorak she was clutching in her fingers.

'It's not for me ... a present for Joseph ... What do you think?'

He thought Joseph would hate it. He thought Joseph would tell her so. He said, 'I don't know, I'm sure', and felt inadequate. It was then he saw the flowered coat. It was seven and six and she had to have it. She counted guiltily the money that Joseph had given her for the shopping, and Balfour on an impulse took out a ten-shilling note and gave it to the stallholder. 'I did see it first,' he said, hoping she wouldn't make a scene.

She was disconcerted but grateful, her face turning pink, her eyes lowered. 'Thank you, thank you very much, Balfour,' she said formally. The flowered coat was made of some kind of velvet. It rippled and shone. It was orange and blue and green and black, with a mustard-yellow ground, and there were buttons small as beads going from wrist to elbow. Balfour thought it was terrible.

He prayed she wouldn't wear it now. He visualised her stalking, swathed in velvet, through the busy market town, the bell-bottoms of her denim trousers flaring out beneath the long and violently coloured hem.

They finished the shopping about five. Dotty had bought a piece of best end of neck so large it could only be carried with difficulty. Balfour thought it wouldn't go in the oven, nor

119

would it keep fresh for long. He bore it stoically along the street with Dotty at his side, the flowered coat slung across her shoulders. He was feeling unwell. His head ached and there was a burning sensation in the pit of his stomach. He refused to admit that it might be another of his attacks coming on. He told himself he was just tired, and perhaps getting a cold. It was six months since his last attack. As he walked, he looked from side to side, as if seeking some safe and dark place in which to hide. He mustn't imagine things, he mustn't let it become worse.

'I think I've got a cold coming,' he said out loud, reassuring himself. Dotty stared at his face and attempted to put her hand against his forehead. She stumbled. The joint of meat slipped from his arms. As he bent to retrieve it, the road broke up under him and he fell on his knees.

'Are you all right?' She was squatting on her haunches, staring at him as she had stared at Willie, with disbelief.

'Fine, fine,' he said with an effort, standing upright, afraid now, sure he was ill. He sensed, rather than saw, the road stretching ahead, the hedges on either side, recently trimmed, the fields beyond, the far distant hills, all permeated by the clear and golden light of the afternoon. There was no darkness anywhere, no feeling of shade, nowhere he might hide.

'I'm so happy,' Dotty shouted, running ahead, the bag of food clutched in her arms, the flowered coat trailing on the road. She wheeled round to face him and the coat flew with her, orange and black. She was like a matador before him, poised on the tips of her feet, hugging the shopping to her breast. She noticed the pallor of his face, the lankness of his hair upon his forehead as if he sweated. She waited till he was almost level and said, 'Balfour.' And he had to stop, for she was planted on the road in front of him. She stood so close to him she must surely hear the thudding in his breast. He could smell tobacco on her breath, see a brown shred clinging to her lower lip.

'Do you want to sit down?' she said. 'You look a bit white.'
He shook his head and they walked on.

'Joseph always says I can't walk anywhere,' said Dotty. 'I can walk ... I can walk miles. Not with him of course ... not any more. We did go for a walk together once, a hell of a long way, talking all the time ... all about children and the future and nice things. When we came to a signpost we just walked right round it – in a circle, still talking – and started back home again.'

Balfour thought everything she said seemed personal and embarrassing. He asked, 'Don't you go walking any more?'

'We don't do anything much any more,' she told him. 'Sometimes we go out in the car round Hyde Park and things ... I quite like that ... except for Stephen Ward.'

'For who?' Balfour was glad now of her chattering. It forced him to keep moving. It postponed the moment when he must lie down at the side of the road.

'Stephen Ward', said Dotty ... 'that poor man. I always think of him when I'm going round Hyde Park. There's so many posh cars and everyone's wearing such expensive clothes ... I keep thinking he must have driven round the park, all dressed up, with Mandy Rice Whatsit beside him. All those parties ... all those weekends in the country. Joseph says he was a victim, a sort of present-day martyr. They used him. Joseph calls him St Stephen.'

'D-does he?' Balfour hadn't meant to shout.

'I don't go that far,' said Dotty. 'I mean, I don't know if he was a victim or not. But he must have thought life was smashing. He felt so in with all that rich crowd and he thought they liked him. When they closed their ranks, he couldn't believe it. He thought he was one of them. Lord Denning said Profumo and that lot were misguided. He said Ward was evil.'

Balfour made some sound, a grunt. The blood pounded in his ears. He held the joint of meat tightly in his arms to stop

121

himself from trembling. The light was growing stronger all the time. It was filling his eyes, obliterating shapes and distances.

Dotty was walking ahead. 'I bet you Joseph hates my coat,' she called. 'I bet you he says something nasty.' She turned to look at Balfour, her face forlorn, her features blurred.

The hedgerows reeled backwards. He said indistinctly, 'Ditch, quick ... quick.'

'What luv? What luv?'

He could feel her arm about his shoulders. She was too heavy for him. She was pushing him to the ground. 'Please,' he begged, his cheek on the surface of the shifting road. 'Please –'

During the afternoon, Lionel went for a brisk walk across the fields, returning via his Mini to take a few sips from the whisky bottle secreted in the boot. Though he wouldn't call himself a teetotaller, he wasn't a drinking man – or hadn't been until his marriage to May. He found increasingly that a small drink gave him the uplift he needed to face her at the end of his day. There was a lot she expected of him – and why not, loving him as she did? He had wanted her to accompany him on the walk, but she had refused, preferring to lie down on the chintz sofa, with only the thumb-sucking and silent Kidney for company. Roland had gone to the stream. Lionel would have liked to show one of them, wife or child, wild flowers, tell them what they were called. There was a certain poetry in the long Latin names. He sat in his hired car, holding the whisky bottle between his knees, the interior darkened by the haystack that towered above the metal roof of the car.

He remembered a childhood holiday taken at harvest time, when he had been allowed to help the men to stook the corn, holding the sheaves upright against his perspiring face while they bound the bundles with thin silver wire – four bundles to a stook. The corn smelt of dried clean paper, scratching the skin of his face, filling his ears with dust. Round and round the bleached white field went the harvester in ever-decreasing circles, the reverse of the stone dropped in the pond, till all that was left was a patch of yellow corn waving slowly in the bald field. The men took sticks, waiting for the rabbits to break cover. He had run with them, leaping over the ground, raising his arm with the peeled white stick held against the sky. The rabbits ran out, lumpy, slower than he thought possible, disorganised and cowardly, so that he closed his eyes lest he should see what he did, beating at the clumsy scattering things. The killed rabbits smelt of nothing, there was no blood. Their eyes soon filmed over and stared straight up at the sky. When hung, they were like sacks of money, all the weight in the belly, swinging and stupid. He hadn't forgotten, even now, that first struggle. It had made more impression on him, that first slaughtering, than the other butcherings he had seen, the human killings enacted in the war. The deaths he had witnessed weren't terrible, only the woundings achieved a degree of brutality. Such killings as he had known had been fragmented, comical – a man blown to bits by a shell, a reconnoitring party of six disintegrated by a mine. No blood, no after-life in death, nothing to show they had been there; in the ragged trees perhaps or strewn about the hedges. The wounded, of which he had been one, had smelt of smoke and excrement, lying swollen or shrunken with eyes screwed up and mouths slack. Spittle at one end and urine at the other. Messy business in the warm and fruitful landscape of Italy.

He put his bottle back into the car boot and climbed over the fence, going slowly across the field back to the hut, threading his way between the grazing cows, looking at their thin legs and their enormous udders.

May was in the barn, alone, changed into a dress of brown linen. It wasn't his favourite dress, it was too short above her knees. She wouldn't speak to him. She bent down to straighten her stockings and he saw the tops of her thighs. He cleared his throat and lay down on the far bed, his arms crossed beneath his head.

123

'What are you following me about for?' she said badtemperedly, flouncing backwards and forwards in front of the mirror.

'But my darling, I'm not. I'm merely resting on this bed.'

'You shouldn't have told your filthy yarns all night,' she snapped. He didn't reply, and she tugged savagely at her limp hair with a pink brush. 'That Balfour heard what you said. Dotty told me. He was absolutely disgusted.'

Still he kept silent. It infuriated her. She wanted to smash things, to set fire to his clothes. Her hair was dreadful, dreadful. She couldn't be seen like this. She rushed at him with face contorted, the pink brush raised to strike him. He caught her wrist just a fraction before the absurd blow came, with his purple cheeks inflamed and his little eyes shining. How close they were, how her moods drew them together. She kicked her plump legs up and down in the air and screamed several times, wrenching at the cravat about his throat, clawing at his chest with her long nails. 'Little spitfire,' he cried, pinning her down, trying to get his arm across the round pads of her knees. She went quiet all at once, her head turned to one side, hair spilled out across the blankets. Roland was shouting somewhere in the field.

She sat upright and pointed bitterly at her stocking. 'Look what you've done.' She bent forward to trace with her finger the ladder that sprang from ankle to thigh.

He couldn't apologise enough. It had been clumsy of him, though there was provocation. She was such a little spitfire. 'Anyway,' he cried, puffing out his cheeks, the colour receding now, placing a rueful hand on his face. 'Look what you've done to me.' He fell back in mock despair with his legs bent at the knee, fondling his scratched face, good-humoured, fortified by the secret nip of whisky.

'Oh shut up, you.' Contemptuous of him, but no longer spirited, she stood up and removed the linen dress, unwearable now by reason of the torn stocking. She peeled the stocking free, exposing pudgy feet, granules of dirt between her piggy toes.

Dotty had dragged the incoherent Balfour behind a hedge. There was no ditch to be found. She had lugged him under the armpits through a gate and propped him against the inner hedge, leaving the shopping bag on the road. He kept asking for a ditch as if they were in danger of being machine-gunned.

She was disturbed at how detached she was in the face of such apparent sickness. She couldn't really bring herself to believe that he was as ill as he seemed. She handled him quite roughly and sat down beside him to smoke a cigarette. He leaned forward over his knees and moaned at intervals, making sounds as if he was going to vomit. She did suggest she might go for help, either to the corner shop two miles on, or further to the hut and Joseph. Balfour shook his head. Dotty lay back, puffing smoke into the fading light.

Balfour was cold. He bent his legs at the knee and tried to curl over on to his side, tried to get his head down into his arms, but nothing obeyed him. Dotty tucked the flowered coat about his legs and sat up. It was almost dark, the field blurring into sky, the light gone from grey to ash, no stars. If a car came she might run out and shout for help. If a car came it would flatten the shopping lying in the road. She climbed the gate, sitting perched there like some bird, staring at a rind of daylight stretched across the horizon.

Balfour was leaning on one elbow clutching the coat about his throat. He spoke in a thin exhausted way. 'I'm so cold, Dotty.'

'Are you better, luv?' She was relieved that he had spoken to her. 'Shall I go for Joseph now? Shall I go for help?' She tried to perceive the expression on his face.

'I must get warm,' mumbled Balfour.

'Yes, luv, of course. We'll get warm, right now. You leave it to me.' She knelt beside him, wrapping the extravagant coat tight against him, pinioning his arms, putting her own arms about his head so that his face was crushed against the denim jacket, the metal buttons like cubes of ice on his cheeks. She herself wasn't comfortable. The spongy grass was soaking into the cloth of her trousers.

'Put the coat over my h-head,' Balfour whined, struggling to free himself, slumping away from her into the grass.

'What coat? Do you want my jacket? Is that what you want?'

'The Joseph coat,' he whined. 'The dreamer's coat.'

She placed it about him like a shawl, tying the arms behind his back to hold it in position, manoeuvring herself so that she was supported by the hedge, stretching him out on the ground with her jacket under his buttocks and his swathed head resting in her lap. 'Is that any better?' she asked hopefully, not knowing what more she could do.

Balfour seemed to be asleep, his face half covered by the coat, his hands clasped together as if he prayed. After a time he said, 'I'm sorry about this. I didn't have time to warn you. It just come on like. No idea when it's going to happen.'

'Oh don't you worry. I don't mind. Honestly. It's quite nice here. I'm quite cheerful really. I'm just thinking about things.'

She didn't really understand what it was that ailed him. He couldn't really explain it himself. The doctors didn't know for sure. Some kind of virus picked up on holiday abroad, some bug in his bloodstream. There was no treatment, no real possibility that he would ever completely recover.

'You mean, like the flu?' she said. 'Only much worse. Something you catch?'

'It's not catching,' he reassured her. 'At least not from me. I caught it all right, but it's sort of dormant in me. It won't pass to you.'

'I didn't mean ...' she said and stopped. She was thinking how Joseph had influenced her, how through him she found sickness distasteful, or thought she did. I do love Joseph, she thought. It was terrible the way he wouldn't let her love him any more. Even after a lifetime of domestic trivia she would still love him, though she wasn't going to be allowed that. It was like the virus stirring in Balfour. She would never completely recover. She would always mourn for what she had lost. What a miserable thing she was, everything suspended by worry and introspection, no laughing or singing or dancing, no trees or flowers. The world was all lovely on the outside, white and green and red, and black as death within. How could she be this way unless it was some disease that gripped her?

She was bending low over Belfour, free of the masculine jacket, wearing a top of some soft woollen material, no bra beneath; he could feel the bounce of her breast against his temple. Dim and dreamy, with a temperature of 103, Balfour craned upwards and kissed her on the lips. He was kissed in return.

'Nice boy,' said Dotty, a little embarrassed and stroking his face with more assurance now that they had been so close. 'Isn't kissing nice. It is nice, isn't it? Are you well enough to go home? It must be awfully late.'

There was one steady stream of wind coming across the black field, blowing hard and steadily right into her face.

He sat up slowly and struggled to his feet, scraping his head against the hedge as he rose. Staggering, he set off down the road.

There was no air in the hut. The wood had burnt quickly and with great heat. Already the pile cut by George that morning had been reduced to ashes. There were only a few logs left on the sofa occupied by May. She quite enjoyed being alone with three men – four, if she bothered to include the peculiar Kidney. It made her feel something of a queen. It was odd Dotty wasn't back yet from the shopping expedition. It was getting on for midnight. Perhaps they had gone to the pictures. Lionel had irritated her earlier by wanting to set off with a lantern to look for them. It was obvious Joseph wasn't worried, only furious she hadn't returned with the food.

George was talking to Lionel about architecture. He said, 'Today the modern architect is a constructor as well as a designer. He can't, however, expect to combine all the engineer's functions as he did before the Industrial Revolution. Contemporary construction is too complex.'

'Quite so,' Lionel said respectfully, fumbling inside the neck of his shirt for the comfort of the penny. The chain had gone. He sat there with his face politely inclined in George's direction waiting for the words to end, for the man's mouth to close.

Gone, but where? It had been about his neck that morning when he changed his shirt. The water he had liberally splashed against his face had run from the edges of the coin down to his belly. He had shivered with the sensation.

'Excuse me,' he said to George. 'I've mislaid something, old boy.' He stood upright, slapping his hands against his stomach, wriggling his knees violently in his creased flannels.

'Been bitten?' Joseph wanted to know, drawing lines on a sheet of paper at the table. He was trying to make a graph of his subconscious. His toil of the afternoon had been of little use in regard to solving the problems of his dream. George had talked to him at length about the use of shoddy materials in housing projects. He had inquired about Joseph's own property and about his ex-wife's flat in Liverpool. He said that some of the property in the cathedral quarter of the city was in a bad state of repair. He said that housing conditions were directly related to delinquency and neurosis. The dream had been pushed from Joseph's mind, to be replaced by guilty thoughts of Roland growing up in the dilapidated city, far away from the green fields and the clean air. Lionel had played with Roland in the field before the boy had been put to bed. May had helped him clean his teeth and combed his hair, telling him he had very smart pyjamas. Roland had looked at her listlessly, without enthusiasm. Joseph had meant to play with Roland himself, but he had been too whacked after the day's exertions to do more than cuddle the boy on his knee.

'What's wrong with you?' May was looking at Lionel standing there with his arms slack at his sides, his mouth open beneath his auburn moustache.

'I've lost something.'

'What?' she said.

'My coin.' He shook his head, crestfallen. 'I had it this morning. I distinctly remember I had it this morning.'

'Oh, that.' She settled herself more comfortably.

'The dead Jerry's Reichmark?' Joseph asked. 'You've lost it? What a bore.'

Joseph wasn't all that attractive, May thought, seeing him above the arm of the sofa, seated at the table with his head bent. Nose too flat and mouth too big. A plum mouth, not attractive in a man. Dotty was a fool, suffering agonies over a man like that. She was just too inexperienced to know that there were hundreds of men to choose from – better than Joseph with his snub nose and his high voice, always going on about education and the meaning of dreams. She let herself remember all the men who had found her attractive. Some of them. It was strange how the good and solid ones evoked no response in her, no feeling of being a woman. All those dreary kindly men, ending with Lionel, wanting to give her security and a nice home – while the other kind, the unstable ruthless ones, who treated her like a whore, slapping her bottom and flinging her on to the bed at the first opportunity, exerted such power over her.

'Lionel,' she said, 'do you remember that day you came home and I was out and I said I'd been to see Christine? Well, I hadn't.'

He looked at her distracted, hardly hearing, trying to think where the coin might be.

'I didn't go to Christine's. I got picked up by a man and went home with him.' Defiantly she swung her foot up and down in the air.

The barn, thought Lionel, that's where it must be. He

129

remembered the tussle with his sweetheart in the barn. He didn't suppose Joseph would like him to go in there now. 'Joseph, old chap', he said. 'Do you think you could possibly come into the barn with me?' He appealed to Joseph, standing there at the table, his face yellow in the lamplight.

'Dear me,' said Joseph, looking up from his paper. 'Do you fancy me, darling?'

May giggled.

'I've got a feeling I left my coin in the barn earlier this afternoon. I'm almost certain. May and I were in there having a little chat this afternoon.'

'Look where you like. It's not my barn,' said Joseph.

'I was thinking about Roland ... being in beddy-byes.'

'Don't you wake him up for God's sake.'

'I'll be terribly quiet.' Gratefully Lionel turned towards the door and opened it and came back again. 'I'll have to take the lamp,' he said apologetically.

May bounced on the little sofa and waved her hands about. 'Oh, sit down. Leave it till the morning. What a fuss about nothing.'

Joseph was looking at Kidney. 'Hold on a tick,' he said. 'I think it's time Kidney went to bed.' He stared at the youth, whose eyes were closed. 'Kidney, do you hear?'

The boy opened his eyes at once.

'Bed for you. Come on.'

Kidney rose obediently at the command and blundered towards the table. 'My pill,' he said. 'Please, my night pill.'

Joseph handed him one, putting the bottle back on the shelf above the door, standing over him while Kidney wiped his face with a flannel and cleaned his teeth. Kidney took a long time, brushing assiduously, gargling and spitting. At last he went out into the night with Lionel, leaving the others in darkness.

'Don't forget to pee,' Joseph shouted, slamming the hut door and finding his way back to the table.

May gave a little squeal in the darkness. She didn't mind being alone with Joseph, but George gave her the creeps. 'Isn't

Lionel awful,' she said clutching her bare toes, bending right over to touch the floor. 'Doesn't he make you sick?'

'Now now, Mrs –' Joseph faltered. 'What's your name?'

'Gosling. Mrs Gosling. Isn't it a funny name.' She laughed, bringing her head up, feeling with her hand the heat of her face. 'Sounds like a duckling.'

'It's Jewish,' George said.

May thought she saw the whites of his eyes, luminous in the blacked-out hut. 'Do you think so? Jewish ... A bit, you mean ... I've often thought that.' She tried to sound polite and chatty. 'His nose, you know ... His grandmother was called Rebecca. I do know that. And that's Jewish isn't it? It's in the Bible.'

George said, 'He's a *Michling*.'

'A what?' she tittered.

'The Nazis had a definition for quarter-Jews,' said George. 'Originally they were exempt from the gas chambers.'

He had a thing about the Jews, that was obvious. May supposed you had to get obsessed by something, if you were like him. He'd probably have a heart attack if someone kissed him.

'I'm a Catholic myself,' she said. 'A lapsed one ... but still a Catholic.' She felt quite intelligent, talking like this to two invisible men. '*Agnus Dei, qui tollis peccata mundi*,' she gabbled, proving her point. '*Christe, audi nos.*' The words had a strange effect on her. She curled up on the sofa and closed her eyes, feeling she was a child again, fearful of the probability that Christ did hear her. What if He had heard what Lionel said last night? Lionel's worry, not hers. 'I'd love a double-barrelled name,' she said aloud, opening her eyes again and looking in the direction of Joseph.

He didn't reply. She could hear him breathing, soft and hurried as if he were running.

'I've got Lionel's blasted penny in my pocket,' she said, glad to confess.

'You're a bit of a bitch,' Joseph said.

131

Lionel entered with the lamp.

'It was on the floor,' he lied. 'Just near the door. Fancy that. Sorry to be a bore about it, but it means a devil of a lot to me, and I just couldn't rest until I had it again.'

'Quite,' said Joseph, humouring him. 'Mrs Gosling's quite a little linguist,' he said, drawing his pencil aimlessly across the square of writing paper, waiting for May to squeal, to pat her hair into shape.

'*Fides quid tibi praestat?*' she murmured modestly, on cue.

Lionel wasn't really paying attention. She would have to give him back his precious token. Later. 'Lionel, you're not listening. I was speaking Latin.'

'You were?'

'I was.' Nasty brutish man tickling his moustache not hearing a word she said.

'What's it mean?' asked Joseph. He looked expectantly at her, and she fidgeted on the sofa, smiling, wondering if she knew.

'It's the baptismal thing ... what the priest says when you're a baby.'

'A baby,' cried Lionel. 'Ah, a baby!'

That had moved him, thought May. He was imagining her in a long white dress with a shawl over her bald head. He was impossible. 'The priest says "What dost thou look for from the Church of God?", and the reply is "Faith", and then he says "What doth Faith assure thee of?", and someone says "Life eternal".'

'Dear God,' Joseph said. 'Life eternal, what a drag.'

'It's true,' May said defensively.

Joseph was quite patient, quite polite. 'I don't doubt some believe it to be true, nor do I doubt they'll be bitterly disappointed. All this love thing is an appalling delusion.'

Lionel wagged a finger at him, speaking with assurance. 'Now, now, love does exist, old boy. It really does.' He mightn't know about architecture, but love – well, he did know about that. 'You may not have been as lucky as myself,

132

but when it hits you ... ah well ...' He shook his head, baffled, as if still dazed by the blow.

'I have been hit by it,' said Joseph. 'Many times as a matter of fact.'

'Ah yes, but really. I mean, really.'

'What do you mean, "really, really". How real can you get? All I know is it passes off. Right off. Sooner or later.' Joseph made a gesture of departure with his hand, slicing the air dogmatically, looking from Lionel to May and back again as if to say their time would come.

Lionel would have none of it. 'I'm a business man myself,' he asserted modestly, 'and I know what I'm talking about. When it hits you, you know. It's no use giving your feelings where they're not appreciated. It pays no dividends. Give them where you will receive an appreciable rate of interest.' He endeavoured to adjust his expression. Try as he might, his mouth widened in a smile. He felt the kind of self-satisfaction and benevolence befitting a man who knew who he was and to whom he belonged.

'Do you believe in love, George?' May asked maliciously, propping herself on her elbow, gazing at the giant on his chair.

'Tolstoy,' observed George, paying no attention to her, 'said that life is all right while you are intoxicated.' He thrust the palms of his hands together, looking at Joseph inquiringly, as if setting a riddle.

'Yes ... well?'

'When you sober up it's impossible not to see it's a fraud.'

'Here's another one,' said Joseph. 'Nothing lasts, absolutely nothing. Neither fear, nor love for one woman.'

'Plato?' suggested Lionel, half fearful.

'No, Marlon Brando.'

Lionel laughed nevertheless, thwacking the side of his leg to show that his sense of humour really knew no bounds.

'Where, oh where, is Dotty?' cried his wife, swinging her legs up and placing the black soles of her feet down again squarely on the rough floor. There was an atmosphere in the

133

hut that made her feel irritable. It was as if they had all been plucked up out of nowhere and set down with the express purpose of being amusing or interesting or something, and they had all been found wanting. It was so embarrassing, not knowing what way to be, Lionel in a tiz about his Co-op penny and Joseph attempting to be profound. She longed for Dotty to return and give them some distraction – ask questions, undo shopping, explain the delay.

George said, 'I'm anxious about Balfour. I feel he may be ill.'

'I shouldn't worry,' said Joseph. 'Dotty can cope.'

'His behaviour of the last few days has been strange. Unlike ... He has been less than himself ... or more. A preparation perhaps.'

'He hasn't seemed very strange to me,' said Joseph. 'What way do you mean?'

'There are currents,' George said. 'Changes ... attitudes ... certain deviations from normal behaviour ... preliminaries ... an increasing impediment in speech.'

'Oh aye,' said Joseph, giving up.

Lionel said he thought he would go and listen to the stock-market closing reports. 'You've got a radio in the car, old boy, haven't you?'

Joseph said he had, that the car wasn't locked, that the knob of the radio was on the floor by the clutch somewhere.

Lionel found himself a candle and a box of matches. When he opened the door of the hut he was too troubled by the loss of his coin to look back at his sweetheart. Like a swimmer, he threw himself from the step of the porch into the field, breast-high in mist, and began to wade to the distant Jaguar.

Though still liable to sudden fits of trembling, Balfour walked without help. The breeze tore free a corner of paper wrapped about the joint of meat. Flap, flap, it went in the night. Slap, slap went his feet on the smooth surface of the road. After a time Dotty could see shapes and grades of darkness – line of

134

hedge, rise of field — even the outline of Balfour's face as he walked at her side.

She wondered if Joseph was worried at her absence. Angry, most likely. She thought she would put in her farewell letter that Balfour had kissed her behind the hedge, that she felt life was exciting. In truth, the embrace of the delirious Balfour, swift though it had been, had only depressed her, illustrating as it did how unexciting life was without Joseph.

'I expect they think we've been boozing,' she said. The road dipped gently down to the stone bridge, to the weeping willow, unseen, rising up out of the stream. The noise of the water coming down from the rocks was deafening.

Then they were climbing the hill again. One more turning to go and a short stretch of road before they came to the gate into the field.

'I'd rather you d-didn't say I've been ill,' said Balfour.

'Don't be daft. What else can we say. It must be nearly midnight.'

'I don't c-care for old G-George to know.'

'Well, I don't care for old Joseph to think we've been doing anything else. Dotty was quite cross and assertive, fortified by their intimacy of half an hour ago. Balfour walked stiffly, with the joint of meat held to his chin. He would just make it back to the hut, to the barn. He would have to sleep there for the night.

'Oh, all right,' she relented. 'I'll say we went to the chippie or something, or that I felt sick. I don't suppose he'll be up anyway.'

Behind the gate the hump of the haystack rose above the two cars. Inside the Jaguar burnt a little light, orange against the blue leather of the seats. Lionel, plump as a Buddha, sat holding his candle aloft, listening to a voice on the radio. They waved at him. He made signs and attempted to wind down the window. They climbed over the second gate, heading towards the hut and were swallowed up in the mist.

In the centre of the field Dotty searched for and found

135

Balfour's hand. Like lovers they stumbled through the damp air.

All alone in the little cabin Lionel sat listening to the market trends. A liturgy of big business, a rosary of abbreviations and percentages, gilt-edged and gold-leafed. Some things were up, some down. Some shaky, some sound.

Awkwardly, with the stub of a pencil he wrote down figures on the back of an envelope. He would wait until the shipping reports, till the announcer said 'Goodnight, gentlemen'. One gentleman to another.

8

Dotty put chairs outside the hut and clapped her hands. 'A photie. Everyone must have their photie taken.'

It was such a perfect morning, she thought, straight out of some woodland scene in a pantomime – a backcloth of shimmering trees, azure blue sky, birds singing. May, encased in white shorts, jaunty as a principal boy, came running from the barn.

'Oh, I hate photographs. I always come out looking ghastly.' Still, she sat herself on the centre chair, rocking alarmingly on the bumpy ground.

It was important to Dotty that there should be some record she could keep of this last time spent with Joseph.

Joseph assembled them on the chairs, Lionel next to his sweetheart, Dotty to the right, clad in her flowered coat, Roland on her knee. Behind, in a row, with arms folded, stood Balfour, Kidney and George.

It wasn't right. After a little thought Joseph asked George to lie down in the grass at their feet, full length, feet crossed at the ankles, his head propped on his hand. In the background, though obviously not included, stood the little timber cabin, windows glinting in the sunshine. With a click of the shutter the images were recorded: the winsome little woman with her smooth knees pushed together, jovial Lionel, Roland with his chin raised and his eyes following the flight of a bird.

Balfour remembered all the other photographs taken of himself by friends of George, copies of which he had never seen. He scowled as Joseph prepared for another shot. Though feeling exhausted, he was no longer ill. George had put him to sleep in the barn the previous night, had removed his shoes and wrapped him in blankets. Throughout he had shown a degree of tenderness that had only registered when Balfour awoke that morning. He found himself unable to look directly at George. George had spent the night in the second cubicle, with the door wide open, so as to be better able to hear Balfour if he cried out. The problems of night travelling, coupled with the technical difficulties of lighting the paraffin lamp, had obliged Lionel and May also to stay in the barn. Their mattress was filled with straw and May had complained of lying awake the entire night.

When Joseph had finished taking photographs they all said that they never looked good in snapshots. Each of them secretly hoped that this time would be an exception. It gave Dotty an odd feeling to think of them all cramped on that little roll of yellow film, stamped together for ever on the wooden chairs, never to get up again. She went indoors with May to make coffee.

George told Balfour he was to lie quietly in the shade for several hours. Balfour said he would do that. George fetched a pillow from the barn and placed it on the grass within the angle of the hut. 'Lie down,' he said, and Balfour rose and lay, pushing his face into the cushion and shutting his eyes.

After a moment George stopped standing over him and walked away down the path.

Balfour turned over and looked up at the summer sky. A wasp droned somewhere above his ear. He got to his knees. The women were still within the hut. He walked a few paces into the bracken near the barn, undoing the buttons of his trousers. A twig snapped. He straddled his feet wider apart. There was a low murmuring in his ears, a dense rise of dust, sunbeams. He flung his arms about his head as if avoiding a

138

blow. A sound like a cat mewing came from between his lips and he spun round, crouching there with his arms held up stiffly on either side of him.

George, walking back along the path, was in time to see him in just this position and Lionel springing upon him, apparently pummelling him about the head with clenched fists. May ran to the doorway of the hut, brought there by the sound of Lionel's voice. It was she, not Balfour, who screamed. She shrank backwards, the round hole in her mouth plugged by her pink-tipped fingers.

The men laid Balfour down with his neck on the pillow and examined his face and chest. First they had to bring his bent arms from about his ears.

'My head,' he said. 'My head.' He felt the skin of his scalp contracting, as a thousand winged insects burrowed into his hair.

'Nothing on your head,' George said, partitioning the black hair, seeing with revulsion the swellings beginning on the pimpled neck. He removed Balfour's shirt and bathed the wasp stings with TCP.

'How awful,' whispered the women.

'Poor devil,' said Lionel hoarsely, feeling his own neck with pity and fear.

Joseph was telling Roland to be careful not to go near the bracken at the far side of the barn. As if it meant something, Dotty took off her flowered coat and stuffed it away in the wicker basket under the sofa. May was terribly distressed. It might so easily have been herself thus violated in the bushes.

The disturbance of the wasps' nest had filled Kidney with unusual energy. He ran from hut to field, scarcely noticed by the others, his whole being flung into activity, cantering heavily through the grass and going down the sloping path. Wishing finally to stop and not able to halt, he ran into a tree; striking his forehead on the bark, he slid to the ground and sprawled there, seeing nothing, his eyes fluttering as rapidly as his heartbeat. He didn't know what had happened to Balfour

139

except that he had opened his trousers in the bushes and that Lionel had struck him to his knees. Joseph had done nothing. Joseph hadn't protested at such violence. A flux of tears came into Kidney's sparkling eyes. He dashed it away with a fierce shake of his head, shouting with lips spitting: 'You horrid man! Rude to undo your trousers. Filthy animal. Should be put away. I'll show you what's what, dirty stinker!'

He fell silent. Someone, Roland perhaps, was calling his name. That much he heard.

Roland stuck out a cheerful tongue and went past him, pretending to have somewhere to go. After a few yards he turned and cried mockingly, 'Daftie Kidney, sitting on the floor.'

'I'm hot.'

'No you're not. You're daft.'

Offended, Kidney hung his head.

Roland saw a piece of glass near his foot and bent to examine it. 'Really,' he said. 'This place should get condemned. It's just dangerous all over.' He settled on his haunches and rocked backwards and forwards. 'Bet you it's clean and safe up there,' he said, jerking his head in the direction of the mountain hidden by the trees.

'Safe where?' Kidney asked.

'Up the mountain. Safe as anything, all clean.'

Kidney got slowly to his feet and with bowed head began to walk back up the path.

'Daftie,' shouted Roland again.

Kidney took no notice. He had some vague idea in his mind that in the hut there was something he wanted, that was safe. Nobody looked up when he entered the door. He put a chair by the sink and climbed upon it, reaching with his fingers for the pills. Finding the bottle he put it inside his jumper, clutching his jumper as he climbed down again. No one saw him.

Joseph was worried by the continuing presence of the nest among the bracken. He pressed George to do something about

140

it. George said there was nothing he could do until dusk.

'What'll you do then?' Dotty wanted to know.

George said he would pour boiling water down the hole.

'That's a bit primitive, isn't it?' asked Joseph. He had thought there was some chemical that could be sprayed at once causing immediate annihilation.

George said he could burn out the nest but it was risky. He hovered between the barn and the hut, keeping a protective eye on Balfour. The others, after a period of adjustment, took sheets and lay down in the sunshine, at the extreme end of the field. It was to give Balfour a sense of privacy.

Lionel had driven his car to the corner shop before breakfast for a morning paper. Now he studied it earnestly and remarked that the country was in a damned mess. Nobody appeared to object or to hold different views. Joseph was lying on his back holding a Penguin book close to his eyes, both reading and shielding his face from the rays of the sun.

May found it difficult to concentrate for long in any one position. She never went brown, only a dull shade of brick. When she bent her legs, sweat gathered behind the folds of her knees. She looked sideways at the sunbathing Dotty, dressed in a swimsuit of dark blue. One arm was curved up above her head, one leg lolled outward from her crotch. There was a little fuzz of blonde hairs catching the sunlight, right at the top of her inner thigh. May felt disgust, almost nausea. It was so immodest. Other women were always revolting. She felt sure Lionel was watching the sprawled girl. Angrily she slapped a fly from her arm.

'Would you like a chair, my sweetheart?' Lionel said, looking up from his newspaper.

She ignored him. She rose to her feet and walked back into the hut, shutting the door behind her. She opened the suitcase still under the table. In the pocket of her trews she found the Co-op penny on its little chain. She left the hut and tiptoed past Balfour with exaggerated stealth. She went a few paces into the bracken and turning from the group at the end of the

141

field lifted her arm, apparently to steady herself.

'Careful, my sweetheart,' called Lionel.

Straightening up, facing in the direction of the barn, she saw Roland standing a few paces from her.

'What did you do that for?' he asked her.

'Do what?' she said, laughing nervously, going to him with her hand stretched out.

'Roland,' shouted Joseph. 'Come away from the nest. I told you.'

Lionel was shaking his head and making sounds of disapproval as he held his paper. 'This man Wilson really is making one hell of a mess, you know.'

'Oh, I love Harold,' cried May, restored, prepared now to be amusing. 'That little duckwing of hair at the back, that solemn northern face. I think he's dishy.'

Her husband smiled at her. 'He's certainly making a dish out of Rhodesia, my sweetheart.'

'I've got room for another toe here,' Roland observed, looking at his foot with interest. Joseph had made him remove his sweater and his jeans and he crouched there in the grass clad in his cotton underpants, shoulder blades prominent, ribs showing, a line of hair, silver in the sunlight, tipping the vertebrae of his spine.

'You're much too thin,' said his father. 'You don't eat enough.'

'I do, I do,' he protested.

'He's not too thin,' May said, thinking he was, dreadfully so, but in some way forestalling a remark, should it be made, on the size and weight of her own body. Protectively she bent over her knees, covering her breasts and small pot stomach. 'Does Mummy give you cod liver oil?' she asked, watching the discomfited little boy who was now plucking at the skin adhering to the cage of his ribs.

'No,' he muttered. 'That's for babies.' He began to struggle into his striped sweater, thrusting his stick-like arms into the air, emerging with hair tousled.

142

'Now, boy,' his father shouted, putting his book face downwards in the grass. 'Don't you take offence.'

'I don't,' Roland replied thickly, struggling with a sense of injustice and the awkward zip of his trousers. Self-pity making his head loll pathetically, he walked across the grass towards the trees.

Joseph reached out a hand and seized him by the ankle as he passed. He wouldn't let go. 'Little softie boy,' he shouted. 'Didums get all cross then? Didums feel a fool?'

Tears flowed down the boy's cheeks. He was both angry and relieved. He beat at Joseph's shoulders with his fists, as hard as he knew how.

They had most of the meat for lunch, the big joint that Balfour had carried from the village. There were potatoes and slices of beetroot. The women ate more than the men, tearing at the fatty chops with sweaty faces and fingers covered in grease.

Afterwards May wanted to go for a drive somewhere into the hills, but Lionel was evasive. Determined to recover his Co-op penny, he had the intention of combing every step of ground he had trodden the previous day. Throughout the meal his hand continually sought the opening of his shirt. Contrite, in that he knew May would have liked to have been taken for a run in the car, but determined not to do so, he dried the plates that Joseph had expertly washed. He took care to keep his head turned from her, lest her expression should cause him to change his plans. Actually May was quite contented. She didn't mind in the least.

There were voices outside the hut. Lionel hovered at the door, thinking it was Balfour, recovered and anxious for food, and saw George talking to an elderly man in a cloth cap. They were nodding and looking in the direction of the bracken.

Joseph said, 'God, it's that Bill, hale and hearty again.'

'Is it Willie?' Delighted, Dotty pranced into the field, holding out her hand, taking the little Welshman by surprise, asking him if he was better, saying it was a treat to see him.

143

Willie removed his cap and nodded at her, bashful.

'He's super. He's a marvellous little bloke,' said Dotty, running back into the hut to confide her opinion to May.

'Is he?' May said, wondering who the man was. When George came into the hut followed by Willie, she still kept her expectant eyes on the doorway, waiting for another visitor.

'This is my friend May, Willie,' Dotty said, pointing at the girl on the settee with sudden pride.

'Pleased to meet you, miss,' he said, taken aback by all the areas of uncovered female flesh.

'Isn't he super,' hissed Dotty, though what it was that so impressed her she couldn't qualify.

May looked at the shrivelled little man. As a child she had spent some time billeted in North Wales and had been early acquainted with pastoral Welshmen who called the cattle home and loved to fondle little girls. She was bored and revolted by him and by Dotty.

'Mr George told me about the nest. Bad that is,' said Willie.

'It was horrible,' cried Dotty.

Roland came in and spoke to his father. 'Can I go for a walk?'

'Burn the nest out, will you?' asked Joseph.

'Most like,' Willie responded, hanging his head and not wishing to sound too authoritative with Mr George there.

'Can I go for a walk with Kidney then?' demanded Roland.

'Nasty business. Lucky it wasn't the boy,' said Willie.

'You're right,' agreed Joseph. 'It doesn't bear thinking about.'

Roland ran out of the hut.

There were blackberries in the hedge – blue-black, juicy. Kidney reached down the high ones for Roland. He ate none himself. Roland dug the stalks out with his nails and stained the pads of his fingers mauve. He rather preferred the red and tight fruits, tart on his tongue; some of the black and ripe ones he let fall on to the road and trod beneath his feet. He could hear the telegraph wires humming, high and quivering above his head. He laid his ear to the warm wood of the telegraph poles and thought he heard the sea. Kidney walked with his eyes looking down at the smooth road, his hands in his pockets. When he plucked the blackberries his eyes lifted no higher than the hedge. They came to the crossroads, one road going right to the market town and the other to the White Horse public house, with the sign hanging motionless in the sunlight and the smithy opposite. The blacksmith was shoeing a cart horse. The horse puffed and the man puffed too, his leather apron touching the ground. A fire glowed in an iron stove. Roland could think only of scripture lessons at school and Pentecostal fire; try as he could he failed to remember the exact meaning of the word. The man went on filing at the raised hoof. Once he cut at it with a short knife and carved away a whole segment of skin. It fell to the stone floor and lay like a slice of coconut. Now and then, fussily, he bent lower, straddling his legs wide, and blew dust from the hoof. Before the shoe was fitted Roland moved away. He couldn't watch the final bearing down, the smell of the horse's foot burning. He wanted to watch, he wanted to stay, but he couldn't.

To the left of the smithy was a church, square-towered. The graveyard was at the back, not seen from the road. There was a signpost saying To the Mountain, as if it was an attraction. The sun burnt on, drugging everything with warmth. Roland would have liked to buy some lemonade at the corner shop but he had no money.

In time the change in the countryside was noticeable. The prolific elms became fewer, the hedges thinned, the lane climbed steeply. At last there were no more houses or cottages. Then the road stopped too. They came to a gate, stone walls at either side. Beyond the gate was moorland, rolling into the distance, purple under a growth of heather. It was vaster, wilder, than Roland had expected – a bleak plateau of flowing earth as far as the eye could see, and the mountain ahead and to the left, one hundred miles away.

145

There was a desert of moorland to cross and a deep valley to descend, not steep but endlessly sloping down to a plantation of firs shaped like an arrow head. Its tip pointed at the black slab of a reservoir and the lower slopes of the mountain. Roland was quite checked by the distance they would have to go. He was at the end of the world; come from any direction start from any place, it would be the same.

The sheep trotted in packs as if they were afraid. When Kidney swung his arms they leapt haughtily, like miniature camels, black muzzles held high. A strange unified cry came from them; they stretched their throats and landed trembling, with ears laid back.

'It's a long way,' said Roland, looking over the edge of the world into the valley that separated him from the mountain.

'Head back, shoulders braced,' bade Kidney, beginning to march across the plateau.

'Have you walked often?' Roland asked, but already Kidney was some way ahead and didn't reply.

Something about the expanse of earth made Roland hungry. He wanted chocolate, biscuits, anything. He shouted to Kidney that he wanted some food badly.

'There's none,' Kidney called, swinging his arms from the shoulder. He waited till Roland should reach him. 'We had a very substantial lunch,' he said sternly, a deep crease between his sleek eyebrows.

'At home,' said Roland, torturing himself, 'We have Mr Mahmood's breasts –'

'Indeed.'

' — of chicken. They're pre-packed and frozen.' Roland gazed at the distant mountain and would have preferred to turn back.

They walked some way across the moor without much purpose, until by chance they found a path, worn through the heather, leading down to the valley.

Roland thought the men who had lived here hundreds of years ago had made the threadbare patch. Kidney said it

146

would be sheep. He was much better in the open air; he replied to most questions when asked. There was a book in the pocket of the sports jacket. Roland could see it above the check flap of his coat.

'What's the book?' he asked, walking behind Kidney, taking care not to tread on his heels, as his father had taught him.

'Joseph gave it to me,' said Kidney.

'Let me see it.'

Kidney reached out the book and handed it backwards. Roland spelt out laboriously, 'John Donne, His Poems.' He turned the pages.

'What's that writing say? I can't read it.'

'Joseph wrote it.'

'What did he write?'

'To my friend Kidney, for whom everything may be possible.'

'What may be possible?' asked Roland.

Kidney didn't answer.

'What's it mean?'

After a moment Kidney paused and reclaimed his book, fingering the open page like a blind man reading braille. 'It means,' he said, 'that he's my friend.'

'What are the poems about?'

'I don't know. I haven't read them.' Kidney put the book back in his pocket and continued the descent into the valley.

Roland looked back the way they had come and already the plateau was shrunk by distance. He could see its surface lit by sunlight, a concave rim of brightness merging into the sky. Below him, quite near, the plantation of firs lay ruptured by shadow.

They had no need to go near the trees. The path wound in a semicircle to the furthermost side of the valley, so that the reservoir in its neat cement sink and the arrow of firs lay to their right and the mountain loomed directly above them. Roland could make out the tower quite specifically now. He

147

was disappointed to see that it was almost a ruin, three walls standing and the fourth gone half way. Pieces of stone jutted like broken teeth out of the ruined mouth of the tower.

It wasn't a difficult climb, hardly a mountain at all now that they were there. The path wound upwards, leading gently to the top. There were even sheep quite near the summit.

'Where are we?' cried Roland, turning round to look out across the valley and the distant fields. 'Where's our hut?'

Frowning, Kidney poised his hands on his plump hips and regarded the view. He could see water a long way off and factory chimneys sticking like upturned glasses from the rim of the sea.

'There's the Estuary of the Dee,' shouted Roland. 'All that bright piece in the sun is the Wirral and Cheshire.'

The tower was quite roomy inside, enough to sit down in. There was a mound of refuse in one corner and some beer bottles. 'What's it for anyway,' said Roland, feeling cheated, kicking the bottles with his foot.

'It's not for anything,' said Kidney, sitting down on a pile of yellow stone, shifting his feet about to balance himself. 'It's a tower for people to see.'

Roland remembered a film he had been to with his grandmother. It had been about a king with a humped back who had drowned his friend in a malmsey butt. 'They put the princes in a tower,' he said, 'but it had beds and things. My dad wouldn't think much of this.' He sat on his haunches and rolled a brown bottle backwards and forwards in the dust.

'King Lear had a beard,' said Kidney.

'Who's Lear?'

'Lear was a king by Shakespeare,' said Kidney.

'How old?' asked Roland.

' – who had some children he wanted to live with. They didn't want him.'

'Why not?' asked Roland.

'He went out for a walk and his beard went white. His good girl came for him and took him home.'

148

'Is that all?' said Roland. He watched Kidney take a bottle of pills out of his pocket.

'Yes,' said Kidney.

'Joseph said you weren't to have those,' shouted Roland. 'You've got to do more exercise.' He reached out his hand and snatched the bottle away from Kidney. He ran to the entrance of the tower, ready to flee down the mountain. He looked back at Kidney, crouched on his seat of stones, dark in the shadows of the interior. 'It's windy up here,' he called, the breeze whipping his hair back from his forehead. 'Why is it windy, Kidney?'

'We're up a mountain.'

'There's towers in the Bible too,' said Roland, leaning his head back and looking up at the square structure. 'There's Babel and Pisa, the leaning one, and there must have been one at Jericho that fell down when the trumpet blew.' He came back into the tower and sat down on the floor, resting his shoulders against the wall. 'Mountains too ... Mount Sinai and the Mount of Olives and the one Moses went up ... things like that. Do you know any mountains in the Bible?' He didn't think Kidney would know any. It had been a rotten story about Lear and his beard.

'Abraham in the Bible took his only son up a mountain,' Kidney said.

'Oh, I know that one.' Roland looked at Kidney who had stood up and turned away from him. 'He only used a ram – only a ram in the end.'

Water was running in a rivulet between Kidney's legs. The stone dust thickened the stream and made it run sluggishly.

'My dad would never sacrifice me,' shouted Roland. 'He doesn't believe in God.'

Kidney was gazing at a sunspot on the stone wall above his head, flickering before his eyes. He felt dazed by the play of light on the crumbling wall. A fly, alighting, clung to a crumb of stonework and crawled into a niche, folding its wings. Kidney turned round, still with his trousers unbuttoned and

149

said pettishly, 'Give me my pills. You have no right.' He tried to tuck himself away, but his hands were ineffectual, inaccurate; he waggled the flaccid member at the staring boy.

'That's rude,' said Roland, looking in another direction and returning fascinated to Kidney and the front of his trousers.

'I want my pills.'

'It's very big. It's bigger than Joseph's.'

'Give me the bottle.'

'I ought to keep the pills. Joseph wouldn't like you to have a pill. You're much too fat.'

Kidney rebuttoned his trousers and stood with arms dangling in the shadow cast by the wall. The fly left its cranny and spun upward into the light. Kidney raised his hands high, palms cupped together, as if he sought to imprison the fly, the spot of sunlight, something.

'Is it the pills that make you so big?' said Roland. 'Is it the pills?'

Kidney wouldn't reply.

'What's your other name?' asked the child. 'What's your real name?'

'A boy like you,' said Kidney, 'oughtn't to be like you are.'

Roland fidgeted in the doorway, not knowing what way he was. He put his face to the wind and blinked his eyes with embarrassment. Still, he wouldn't give up the bottle of pills.

Going down the mountain, he tore from the bracken a piece of heather for Joseph. It was dried up, like the lavender his mother kept in the linen drawer. He held the bottle in one hand and the odourless heather in the other, following Kidney down into the valley.

'What's the pills called?' he asked Kidney.

Sullenly Kidney told him they were Phenobarbitone. 'They sedate me,' he told Roland, turning his face to the boy higher up the path. The child didn't know what he meant. He held the bottle tightly in one clenched hand.

'Pheno barbitone,' sang Roland. 'Pheeeno barbeeee tone.'

It was from the Italian, like vista, and only half sad, the

150

other half funny. He sang the strange words over and over, shaking his head from side to side, the breeze carrying the name away ... 'Pheno, pheeeeeno, pheno-bar-be-tone.'

Half way down the mountain he unscrewed the bottle cap and with difficulty swallowed one of the oblong capsules. He could feel it lying against his throat, cold, obstructive. He sucked in his cheeks and collected saliva under his tongue, using it to wash down the pill.

At the far side of the valley, before the ascent to the plateau, he took two more. He took a fourth when he turned to look back at the mountain, blackening now and the tower a smudge against the whitening sky. He swallowed ten capsules in all, the last before they went through the gate. Ten, he reckoned, would be enough to put a lot of weight on him and make him tall and strong. Perhaps not all at once, but in a matter of days. He was only a little worried by what he had done. His mother had repeatedly warned him about aspirin and the tablets she took when she couldn't sleep. They were a different kind of pill, he thought, pills to make you better when you were ill, not like Kidney's pills, which were just to make him grow.

He was glad Joseph had stayed at home. The mountain had been a bit of a let-down. Only an old ruined tower, no battlements, no peep-holes, nothing, just a lot of old beer bottles.

Joseph would have yawned.

Balfour woke at teatime and was sick in the grass.

He raised his white face and saw the sunbathers at the end of the field, Joseph and Dotty and May. He went inside the hut to swill out his mouth and Dotty ran over the grass after him.

She looked at him with interest and wanted to know how he felt.

'Fine,' he told her. He spat into the sink and did feel better. His face was a mess. The stings and constellations of pimples

151

were merged. His eyes were large with fatigue. 'Where's George?' he asked her.

'Painting the house. Ma and Pa MacFarley's windowsills. Gone off with Willie.'

'I've been sick in the grass. Threw up, like. I wouldn't w-want him to see.'

She offered to clean it up. 'Honestly, I don't mind,' she said, looking about for a bucket. She still felt a doctor should have been called. It frightened her, someone being sick and stung about the head by wasps. Finding a pail under the sink she went out purposefully, ignoring Balfour's protests, thinking of the nuptial flight of the queen of the hive and the fertilising male plummeting to the earth. Serve him bloody well right, she told herself giggling, looking about for Balfour's vomit in the grass.

When she returned she had to tell him about the bees, the little she knew, while she made him some tea. 'At the very end, at the very end, the toughest bee, the one that flies high enough to mate the queen – why, he leaves most of himself inside her and drops dying to the ground.'

'Is that so,' said Balfour, depressed by the cruelty of it.

Gaily she poured him out a cup of tea. She wouldn't call the others in – why should she? 'It's silly, isn't it?' she said, handing him the sugar. 'What a way to go.' She laughed quite loudly and he laughed with her. She felt at ease with him, elated. She kept smiling. He felt there was a definite relationship being established between them, something special. It was a shock when she told him she was leaving early in the morning.

'Leaving ... where?'

'I'm going to London ... or home.' She stared self-consciously at the cups and saucers. 'I'm not sure where I shall go. Obviously I can't stay here.'

'No, of course not,' he agreed, not finding it at all obvious, disappointed that she wouldn't be staying longer, that they weren't going to know each other better. It annoyed him that he should feel distressed, before there was anything to feel distressed about.

'I just can't hang about here ... now.' She leaned back in her chair, playing with the limp strands of her hair. 'I mean, I can't hang about now.'

For one moment, he thought, she might mean because of him kissing her in the field. He half believed it, but he knew it wasn't that.

'I mean, it's obvious he doesn't want me. It is ... isn't it?' She looked at him for a denial. They were both tentative, both disappointed, though she was the more cheerful.

'I suppose so,' he said.

'I don't know why I've stuck it so long,' she admitted. 'Honest, I don't know why. I don't really want to go, but I must.' She jumped to her feet. 'I'll give you my address, my home address, and I'll write to you and we'll keep in touch.'

'Yes, we could do that all right,' said Balfour, without hope.

'You won't mention to anyone that I'm going to do a flit, will you?' Dotty turned to him earnestly. 'You won't, will you?'

'N-not a word. I'll carry your suitcase if you like.'

'Would you? Would you really?' She hadn't really thought she would go. Still, if Balfour expected her to leave and wanted to carry her suitcase she supposed she would have to go.

'I hope we meet again,' he said dejectedly.

'Oh, we'll meet,' she said carelessly enough. 'If not on earth, then somewhere else.'

When George came back with Willie he spoke sternly to Balfour. 'You ought to be resting,' he said. Balfour, anxious not to appear ungrateful for care given, lay down obediently on the sofa.

Willie smacked his lips and made sympathetic noises. 'And you not too well,' he said, his eyes moist with satisfaction. 'I hear you took bad last evening, had one of those attacks. Very

153

sorry to hear it ... that and the wasps.'

Joseph came indoors, skin glowing. He showed his burnt chest to Dotty. 'Look at that, Dot-Dot. How's that, eh?'

'Smashing,' she agreed, turning her head away from his fiery breast and the two nipples embedded like black pips. 'Why hasn't Roland come back?' she said.

He buttoned his shirt neatly and shook his head, 'Don't ask me. He's down at the stream, isn't he?'

'Is he?' She wouldn't tell him. She put more water in the kettle and averted her eyes from his sunburnt skin.

He went slowly out into the field, glancing at Lionel, who was still reading his newspaper.

'Roland,' he called, 'Roland.'

'He's gone for a walk with that Kidney,' May told him.

'A walk – are you sure?'

'He asked you if he could go. Several times in fact.'

Joseph studied the trees and sniffed the air. 'Extraordinary,' he said. 'Well, they can't have gone far.'

'They've been gone hours,' May said cruelly. She followed him into the hut and sat down at the table, watching Dotty put out more cups.

'Balfour's better,' Dotty said, nodding in the direction of the sofa.

'Is he? What's been wrong with him?' asked Joseph, standing at the window looking out at the field and the sprawled and lonely Lionel.

Balfour kept his eyes closed.

'Don't you think it's a little foolish letting Roland go off with Kidney?' May said.

'Foolish? What's that supposed to mean exactly?' Joseph faced her, knowing exactly what she meant, angry, fearful that he might be put in the wrong.

'Well, Kidney's not exactly a suitable companion for a little boy. He's very odd.'

'Odd?'

'Yes, odd.' May turned to Dotty for support. 'Do you think Kidney's fit to look after Roland?'

Dotty looked at Joseph and was forced unwillingly to defend him. 'I don't think there's much harm in him ... He's a bit simple, but he's all right.'

'Kidney isn't simple,' Joseph said sternly. 'I've told you that often enough.' He was sorry at once that he had spoken so loudly. She had meant to be loyal. He added more gently, 'He's not simple at all. He's just mentally blocked. He's perfectly intelligent and normal, but he can't communicate.'

'That's not what you said before,' said Dotty.

'Perfectly normal!' May lifted her eyebrows and eyed him incredulously. 'He's almost an imbecile. There's nothing normal about him.' She was growing irritated, malicious. Savagely she dug her nails into the table top. She couldn't bear Joseph and his supercilious ways, and Dotty rattling the cups, and the ridiculous wooden hut set in the middle of nowhere. 'I think it's terrible,' she cried. 'A little boy like Roland, sleeping in the same room as that big fat man and going off for walks with him for hours ... Anything could happen. He looks as if he's abnormal.'

Joseph thought she was absurd. 'You don't know what you're talking about,' he told her sharply. 'I'll just walk over to the road and look for them.' He glanced at Dotty, but she wouldn't look at him. She blamed him too.

'I'll just s-stretch my legs a bit,' said Balfour, rising from the sofa and coming to the door. 'I'll just come over the field for a walk.'

They passed Lionel in the grass, the newspaper lying flat, his head propped on his arm. He was snoring.

'I shouldn't worry,' said Balfour. 'They won't have gone far.'

'I'm not in the least bit worried,' Joseph told him. 'That woman's a cow.' He shook his head with disgust. 'It doesn't do to coddle them too much, you know. They've got to have a

155

feeling of independence. Strike out on their own, dear boy.'

Balfour agreed, keeping pace with difficulty, thinking of Roland being independent, striking out with his mentally disturbed companion. 'We've got quite a few lads l-like Kidney at the club,' he said. 'Same types, same difficulties, only a bit more predictable.' He looked quickly at Joseph but failed to read his expression.

Joseph said abruptly, 'How so?'

'Well, you get to know the signs. It's a kind of pattern. They've got the same troubles at home, lack of interest, lack of –'

' – security?' suggested Joseph.

'That and other things ...'

'What things?'

'B-bad housing. Three or four to a bed. Bad diet. Bad schools. They usually have mentally defective parents and a long history of –'

'Kidney's parents are perfectly intelligent,' said Joseph. 'Particularly about Kidney.'

'Yes – well, there are differences,' Balfour conceded. 'Different environment, like. As a general rule there's only one parent anyway. The dads have usually b-buggered off somewhere.'

His head was aching once more. The poison was working through his bloodstream. But he would gladly have been stung all over again if it would have erased that last remark. 'I only meant about the lads at the club. I mean the parents are different ... You and Roland, that's different. I can see that ... You understand him.'

'I love him,' said Joseph simply, coming to the gate at the end of the field. He climbed it agilely and walked quickly away along the path between hedge and hay-stack.

Roland, turning the bend of the road, saw his father at the entrance of the farm and began to run towards him with arms held out. Swaggering, Joseph went leisurely to meet his son. The boy ran swiftly, clutching the sprig of heather.

156

'Where the devil have you been,' Joseph shouted. He swung the child up in his arms, shaking him fiercely. 'Where have you been, beauty boy? Just where have you been?'

Roland was trying to tell him. He was choked with the violence of the embrace and the excitement of his return. 'We've been up the mountain,' he got out at last, looking up slyly at Joseph's face, waiting for the surprise to show.

'Up the mountain!'

'Me and Kidney, right to the top. We did, didn't we?' He twisted in his father's arms seeking confirmation from Kidney.

'All that way?' Joseph was amused and delighted. He turned and called triumphantly to Balfour. 'Did you hear that, eh, Balfour? Would you believe it, right up the mountain.'

Balfour said 'Jolly good', looking at the animated child and the silent Kidney scuffing his boots at the edge of the road.

Roland rode on Joseph's shoulders across the field, a conqueror's return. He beat at his father's head with his fists and felt giddy. The sky was colourless now, without clouds. It was like riding on the back of an elephant, swaying high above the ground, with Balfour and Kidney following, lurching under the low branches of the elm tree, the sky rocking up and down, his heart bumping. He hoped he wasn't going to be sick.

They were all amazed at him. Roland was gratified by their surprise. Dotty made him fried eggs and tomatoes, but he was no longer hungry. He drank several cupfuls of water, but his throat remained dry. 'It was lovely up the mountain,' he said, attempting for Dotty's sake to eat something. 'You could see all the way to Liverpool ... and the sea shining.'

'What about the tower?' Dotty wanted to know. 'Was it a real tower?'

'Yes. It was jolly good.' He looked at his father and said quickly, 'It was a super tower, really good ... One of its walls had gone. Wasn't that interesting? Kidney told me a story about a king and some children.'

157

'Did he now?' Joseph made sure that May had heard. 'Kidney told you a story did he?'

'Eat your supper,' said Dotty, not wanting the food to be wasted.

'All about this Lear going off for a walk. It was a good story,' lied Roland. He dropped his hands into his lap and yawned. 'I don't want any more egg, thank you, Dotty.'

'You mean King Lear?' said his father.

'What?' The child pushed his plate away. The light in the hut had almost gone. His father's face was in shadow. 'Kidney showed me his wee-wee,' he said. 'It's awfully big.' He yawned again, his eyelids heavy.

Lionel laughed and wished instantly he hadn't. You never knew quite where you were with Joseph, all unconventional and bohemian one moment and prudish as they come the next. Lads often did that sort of thing among themselves. Nothing to be shocked about. Perfectly understandable. Of course Roland was a little young and Kidney a little old, but even so. He looked at his wife and was deceived by the expression on her face. He touched her leg with his knee and kept his mouth solemn.

'Did he?' said Joseph, regarding the child a moment longer before rising from the table to light the lamp.

May longed to interrogate Roland but was intimidated by the presence of Joseph. She felt uneasiness at the situation not yet explained and satisfaction that her fears had been justified. She looked at Kidney contemptuously.

Roland's throat hurt. He found it difficult to talk. 'My mouth feels funny,' he complained, letting his jaw go slack.

Joseph told him he was tired. 'You've been a long way, little soldier. It's time you were in bed.' Gently he undressed the boy, wiped his fingers with a flannel and dabbed at the smooth, sleepy face. 'There,' he said. 'That's my beauty boy.'

Roland was too tired to do his teeth. Joseph insisted. The child began to cry. 'I don't want to ...'

Joseph disliked the whining protest. He flung down the

158

toothpaste in irritation. 'Oh don't bother then. Let them all fall out,' he shouted.

'He's tired,' said Dotty, wanting to take the weary boy on her knee, but not doing so.

Lionel took Roland to the barn. It was still and silent out in the field. No breeze, the trees motionless, the sky waiting for the moon. 'Must be careful of the wasps' nest,' said Lionel. 'We mustn't trip over that, must we?'

Roland was too drowsy to be frightened. Besides, the man's strong arms held him sure and safe. His own body felt strange, heavy. Even the tips of his fingers lying on the curve of Lionel's wrist were leaden and insensitive. He was carried into the barn and laid down.

'Good-night old boy,' said Lionel, tucking the blankets about him firmly. He rested on the side of the bed and brushed the hair away from the boy's unseen forehead. 'No tricks tonight, old boy. No pennies in your ear tonight.' The child spoke so indistinctly that Lionel was forced to lower his head on a level with the bedclothes. 'What's that, old boy?'

'May put your penny down the ...'

'Down where?'

' ... wasp hole.'

'*May* did?'

But the child slept. Lionel strained forward to catch a glimpse of his features, but the darkness was tight and final.

He rose at last and walked outside, closing the door behind him. He stood as near to the bracken as he dared. It was so still out there under the trees that he fancied he could hear the wasps moving, like honey trickling, in their nest beneath the leaves. May had thrown his coin down there, May had done that? He didn't doubt Roland.

Through a triangle of light shining from the porch a man passed, plodding heavily in the darkness. Lionel listened to the footsteps going over the grass and when the sound finished went back into the hut.

'Gone down all right?' asked Joseph, wanting peace,

159

distressed by his angry parting with Roland.

Lionel nodded, not looking at May, going to the sofa to sit beside Balfour.

She knew something was wrong. His face had in some fashion collapsed. Only his moustache seemed permanent.

'Asleep, is he?' persisted Joseph, moving restlessly about the hut.

Lionel nodded once more and fiddled with the cravat about his throat.

'I've sent Kidney for the milk. I thought I'd meet him on the way back and have a bit of a talk with him.' Joseph wasn't concerned about their opinion of Kidney, only of himself. I've spoiled it all, he thought: Dotty's holiday – poor Dotty, slouched over the table rolling her cigarettes – and Roland's. He suppressed the desire to go now, at once, to the barn and tell the boy he was sorry about the tooth-brushing.

May sensed he was vulnerable. She couldn't help taking advantage. 'You really ought to have a little talk with Roland. You'd get more information out of him. Anything might have happened, you know.'

'I don't see it would serve any purpose.' Joseph tried to be patient.

'Boys of Kidney's age are very developed nowadays,' said May. 'Normal ones, let alone that one –'

'If you're trying to suggest Kidney assaulted Roland –'

'Well, what did he want to show his thing to the child for?' asked May. She gave a little giggle and Joseph said quickly, 'All adolescents experiment ... If he had harmed Roland, Roland would have told us.'

'If he was my child ...' began May, tossing her head.

'Well, he isn't, is he?' he retorted.

Balfour was disturbed. He was convinced now that they were all different from him, even the foolish May. They must know more, they appeared to know more. Behind everything, they said, lay something else, another meaning altogether. They had such tolerance. They didn't think it all that

160

important that Kidney might have exposed himself to Roland. Even May's comments were made only to get at Joseph – she wasn't concerned about the child. And Joseph, why was he worried about the effect on Kidney? Taking a broad view, he was right to worry about that; but there was something wrong in it all. There was family, and blood ties, and sticking up for your dad even if you did think he was a right yob of a bastard, and not letting on you had no underpants and telling the rent man your Mam was out when all the time she was hiding behind the back door, and when it came down to the centre, the core, all the feuding and protecting was pride in your own flesh and blood – well, maybe not pride, but loyalty: there wasn't anything else. But somewhere along the line Joseph and Dotty and the rest of them, old George too, had cut themselves free from that sort of thing, gone out on a limb. They didn't really feel they belonged to anyone any more.

'One has to be very careful,' Joseph was telling him – it was Balfour he was looking at – 'not to suggest too much to a child. One must guard against meddling.'

'Well, he looked a bit pale to me,' May cried, unable to keep quiet. 'Not at all well.'

'Rubbish. He was just tired. All that way up the mountain. He's only a child.'

'He looked more than tired. He didn't eat any supper.' She was holding the sprig of heather, rolling it back and forth across the palm of her hand, rubbing the dry buds from the stem.

'That's mine,' Joseph cried, snatching the heather from her and sticking it into the pocket of his shirt. He flounced out of the door. They heard him shout a greeting, and then a farewell, and Willie's voice replying 'All the best, all the best', as if it were Christmas.

Lionel was watching his wife sitting in her chair, separate from him, head lowered to scrutinise her polished nails. Beneath the darkening roots of hair lay her little pale-grey brain, hidden, secretive, beyond his reach or influence. His

161

vicious wife. How often had he met old comrades from the regiment who seemed at first the same comrades, untouched by time. Only later, after some conversation or longer acquaintance, one found they weren't the same but altered beyond recall. They had taken up smoking or given up drink, learnt to drive or become religious, adopted a new style of speech, an unfamiliar mannerism. The same yet no longer the same. People changed and in changing affected others, were affected in their turn, a continual process of addition and subtraction. Cut the communication lines and contact was broken, no information could come through. If the breach was serious enough, the lapse of time long enough, one could be fired upon by one's own guns.

9

Joseph waited at the stile for Kidney to return with the milk. He stood listening to the trees shifting in the darkness. When he heard Kidney blundering towards him, he called out, 'Is that you?'

Kidney had stopped in alarm, but recognising the familiar voice he advanced again. 'I've got the milk,' he said. 'I didn't drop it.'

'Now look here, my boy,' shouted Joseph. 'I want some straight answers. What did Roland mean?'

There was no reply.

'You remember what he said,' cried Joseph. 'Don't pretend you didn't. He said you showed him your ... wee. Those were his words.'

'Yes,' said Kidney.

'Well?' demanded Joseph. He wanted to strike the fat youth across the face.

'I didn't show him,' said Kidney. 'In the tower I went to the toilet. He looked.'

Joseph felt enormous relief, and anger that he had been forced by the others to submit the boy to such questioning. Of course it hadn't been as they had imagined. There had never been the remotest possibility. 'Right you are,' he said. 'That's all I wanted to know. Over you come.'

But Kidney remained on the opposite side of the stile.

'Come on, boy. Move yourself.'

'He took away my pills,' said Kidney. 'He said you wouldn't like me to have them. You do let me have them, I said.'

'What pills?' Joseph couldn't wait to return to the hut and berate May for her stupidity.

'They told me I should take them every day ... he kept them in his hand.'

'Your pills are in the hut,' said Joseph. 'I put them somewhere yesterday.' He hadn't the patience any more to talk to Kidney. It was too exhausting. One step forward, two steps back. Impatiently he bade Kidney hurry up and waited for him to climb the stile and descend heavily into the field.

At the porch Joseph changed his mind. He stumbled in the direction of the barn. Spreading out his arms, he felt with his hands along the rough wall to the pane of glass. No sound within. Voices from the hut, water running in the sink, the trees shifting below in the Glen. It wasn't much use going into the barn, it wasn't as if he could see anything. He would take a candle over later. Kidney was still standing in the porch, the milk bottles clutched to his breast.

George was frying something at the stove. He turned with pleasure to greet Joseph. 'Got them all done,' he said.

'Jolly good,' said Joseph, not knowing what he was on about. He tried to remember where he had put the bottle of pills.

'My father's windowsills are white,' George declared, turning a piece of bread in the hot fat.

Joseph ran his fingers along the edge of the shelf by the cooker and knocked a box of matches to the floor.

'First we burnt off the old paint. Then we sanded. Then we undercoated,' George said.

'Good, good,' said Joseph, looking about him. Of course the pills were on the shelf above the door, along with the hammer and the tins of paint. He reached up with certainty, remembering clearly how he had placed them. They weren't there.

164

Dotty saw his expression. 'What's wrong?' she said quietly. 'What's wrong, love?'

'What?' He glanced at her angrily, unable to hear her above the noise of the fat spitting in the pan.

'What's wrong?' she repeated. 'Was it your little talk with Kidney?' Her face glowed with a kind of expectancy.

'For God's sake stop muttering. I can't hear a damned word you say.'

It was so unfair of him. She set her mouth in a tight line of inward suffering and fiddled with the ends of her lank hair. Offended, she turned her face in Balfour's direction, so that he might see her humiliation.

May was trying to be nice to Kidney. 'Please,' she begged him. 'Do tell me the story about Lear, the one you told Roland.' She was thinking maybe it was a pretty odd story at that, not quite like Lionel and his temple but along those lines.

'A king,' said Kidney promptly, 'had nowhere to go, and his three children were cruel to him, but the youngest one –'

'I think I'll just go for a breath of air,' Lionel said abruptly, rising from the sofa and making for the door.

May was uneasy at his attitude, his prolonged detachment. He looked, she thought, ill, shocked. Surely he wasn't worrying about Kidney showing his thing to the child? The man was so inconsistent. She was annoyed that he might be concerned about someone other than herself. 'Well, bring back the whisky you keep hidden in the car,' she said spitefully. 'We'd all like a drink.'

Out he went without a word, without even a reproachful glance.

' ... then his nice daughter came for him and looked after him for good,' Kidney was saying.

'Is that all?' she asked, disappointed.

'No, it isn't,' Joseph said loudly, delving into the covers of the sofa. 'Move,' he bade Balfour curtly.

'Well, what else?' inquired May, wondering why he couldn't sit still but always had to be tidying things.

'When he finally did go off with his daughter somebody killed her by mistake. It was an accident, but his fault.'

'How dreadful.' May followed Lionel in her head, stepping uncertainly through the field.

'It wouldn't have been right,' said Kidney, 'to have told Roland that. I knew it, but I didn't say it.'

Joseph sat down on the sofa and looked sideways at the uncomfortable Balfour, as if to say 'Isn't that remarkable?' Beyond Balfour's ear he glimpsed Roland's clothes neatly folded for the morning, laid down on the stove. He rose again and sat on the stove top, feeling with his hands behind his back for the outline of the pill bottle in the pocket of the boy's shorts. No, not there. He went to the sink and took up the stub of candle used by Lionel the previous night.

Curiosity overwhelmed Dotty. 'What are you doing now?'

He told her he was going to have a look at Roland.

'What for? What's wrong?'

He shouted at her now. 'Because I bloody well choose. Mind your own blasted business.'

For a moment she was infected by his anger. 'I *will* mind my own bloody business,' she said. 'I *will* mind it ...'

But already he had gone from her out of the door.

'You've forgotten your blasted matches. God,' she screamed, running after him and flinging them into the pool of grass. Then, spent, she came back into the room and sat down at the table, banging her two fists impotently against her bony knees, the colour leaving her cheeks.

No one spoke. May was smiling, turning the diamond ring round and round her finger.

'I shall go tonight,' said Dotty, forced to speak. 'I shall go now and not wait for the morning.'

'That's right,' said May, not really caring for the idea. It placed her and Lionel in an isolated position.

'I must go at once,' Dotty said loudly, looking at Balfour.

'Ah yes,' he said, embarrassed by her impulsiveness and the presence of George.

166

She seized him by the hand and dragged him to his feet. She was pulling him toward the partition. 'I must pack my clothes,' she cried. 'My clothes and my lovely coat.'

'Steady on,' he said, stepping into the cubicle with her, feeling foolish as she closed the partition and bound them in darkness.

'Balfour, I do have to go ... You do see that. I'm terribly sorry –'

'It's none of my business,' he told her awkwardly. 'It's nothing to do with me.'

He didn't see why she was apologising to him. It wasn't him she was leaving.

Outside in the room May was telling George that the air was very fresh in the countryside. 'So fresh and breezy,' she said, detesting Lionel for going off and leaving her with the giant.

George put his plate into the sink and came to sit at the table, looking at her with that melancholy expression on his face. He said nothing.

'You're used to it, of course. Me, I'm knocked out. All this marvellous air.' There was daft Kidney staring at her with his skin coloured like a rose. 'I think it's just beautiful round here ... so peaceful.' The way George never answered upset her dreadfully. She couldn't bear his long sorrowful face and those sloe-shaped eyes. He always seemed to be judging. She fidgeted in her chair. She could hear Dotty opening drawers in the cubicle and Balfour's voice, hesitant and muffled. The girl was quite mad, rushing off in the middle of the evening without transport. It was unforgivable of her to leave Lionel and herself alone. She told George she thought Dotty was mad. Still he chose not to speak. She said rudely, 'I'll keep quiet, if you like.' It was like talking to a brick wall.

The partition of the cubicle was pushed back and Dotty came into the room with her suitcase. Self-consciously Balfour stood behind her, blinking in the light of the paraffin lamp.

'Well, I'm off now,' said Dotty, standing there with her

suitcase. She had hoped Joseph would have returned in time to prevent her departure. She had very little money and there were no buses going anywhere.

'Don't forget your hat,' the smiling May told her, thinking how silly the girl was, how irrational. Fancy letting a man upset you so much that you were forced to walk about the countryside all night. She hoped Dotty wouldn't meet Lionel in the field and ask him to drive her to the village.

Putting the black sou'wester on her unkempt hair, making a clumsy gesture of farewell. Dotty went out of the hut. She was surprised to see a full moon, white as milk, risen above the trees, bathing the field in light. How bright it was, how romantic. The size of her nose wasn't important. She could see the delicate glimmer of the young birch trees lining the path down into the Glen.

Joseph had lit the stub of candle and placed it on the washstand. The barn was cluttered with beds: the one that had done duty as a litter for the collapsed Willie propped on its end against the far wall, Kidney's bed, Balfour's mattress still on the floor, blankets crumpled, the cot shared by Lionel and May. He had to climb over the cot to reach his son.

The child lay on his stomach with one hand raised in protest against the pillow, face turned sideways. When Joseph stooped down to smooth back the hair from the boy's brow the skin was cool to his touch. Roland slept peacefully. In the morning he would wake refreshed and they would go down to the stream together and he would say where he had hidden the bottle of pills and why he had done so. It had only been a childish prank. Relieved, Joseph snuffed out the candle flame between his fingers and shut the barn door. There was Lionel walking across the grass.

Lionel had encountered Dotty behind the stile and had shaken her hand formally. He had expressed no surprise that she was leaving, nor did he offer to drive her anywhere in his

168

car. He was in a no man's land. 'Take care of yourself, my dear. Mind how you go.'

'Yes, I'll do that.' Awkwardly she had nodded her head and let go of his hand. 'Please tell him I'm sorry,' she called impulsively. 'Please tell Joseph I love him.' But already he was climbing the stile and he didn't turn his head.

It's true, she thought, wading the shadow of the haystack and seeing the road set like a river between the hedgerows. It's the truth that I love him. Still, she was glad to be free – if not yet emotionally, then geographically. A great burden had been lifted from her. The relief was such that she imagined that if she spread her arms she might yet fly above the ground. She had escaped. She swung her suitcase back and forth and began to skip along the luminous road.

10

May had seen Lionel approaching from where she stood at the window. She could hear him talking to Joseph, gravely, all the bounce gone out of him. She cried out sharply, 'Did you get the drink, Lionel?'

'There wasn't any whisky,' he said, entering the hut.

George boiled a kettle of water and carried it outside to the bracken. He rested the kettle on the grass and squatted on his haunches, probing with his fingers for the exact location of the wasps' nest.

Kidney stood in the doorway and watched George curiously, looking at his great boots that reflected the moonlight and the metal kettle that glittered in the undergrowth. When George poured the water down through the tangle of leaves and fern, Kidney raised one arm above his eyes as if avoiding a blow. He didn't understand what was happening. He moaned, overcome with dread, rubbing his arm against his eyes. Joseph shook him by the shoulder and asked him what was wrong. He looked beyond the distressed youth to George and told Kidney there was nothing to fear.

'Dotty's gone,' said Kidney. 'She ran away. She took her hat.'

'Oh.' Joseph shrugged and turned away, hardly concerned. She wouldn't go far.

When he came back in with the kettle, George suggested

they should play another game of Monopoly. He looked from one to another of their faces. 'I should enjoy it,' he said in his calm and weary manner.

Joseph had involuntarily shaken his head in refusal. He stood in the centre of the room and said undecidedly, 'Well, if you feel like that –'

George said he would fetch some paraffin from the store shed first, as the lamp was burning low. 'Set the game,' he told May, taking up the polythene container from beside the cooker.

'Shall we?' she asked, once he had gone, looking to Balfour for a decision. Joseph had climbed on to a chair and was searching the shelf carefully.

'Hold the lamp up for me,' he told her, and she did as he asked, keeping it away from her face, disliking the smell of the drying wick.

'Roland took my pills,' Kidney said, watching them both. 'He took away my bottle.'

Joseph looked down into the upturned face of May, the calculating eyes softening with alarm, the mouth, black under the held-aloft lamp, opening to shout an accusation, a criticism. 'Rubbish,' he said. 'They're about somewhere.'

The harsh tone of his voice and the contempt in his eyes silenced her. She set the lamp on the table and bent her head to hide her feelings, which were mixed. She was instinctively certain that Kidney had given the child the pills. She thought Joseph was a fool, he would dismiss as nonsense anything she might say. Well then, let him take the consequences.

Balfour told himself there was nothing to worry about. Kidney had stolen the pills and was trying to blame Roland. Kidney had hidden them somewhere so that he could take his three prescribed tablets a day. Mental defectives, like the old, clung to established routines. It gave them security.

Lionel looked as if the loss of the pills was a personal insult. They were all, he thought – all of them – irresponsible and undisciplined.

171

May set out the Monopoly board and counted the money. When it was done Joseph demanded that she make a cup of tea. She did as he asked without a comment; she could afford to be compliant now that she knew he was to be shown up as a fool. She dwelt with pleasure on the thought of his discomfiture the following day when Roland would be sick and petulant and wanting to go home to his mother. She looked at Lionel, but he wouldn't return her glance. She put the cups noisily on to the table, rehearsing what she would tell Lionel when they were alone. I object to your attitude ... How dare you treat me like this ... Everyone noticed what a bore you were about Churchill ... George says you're a Jew ...

There was very little sugar left in the basin. Hardly enough for one person. Joseph said Kidney ought to have the spoonful that remained.

'Ought he?' said May grimly.

'Take it, Kidney,' ordered Joseph. 'You've got a sweet tooth, I know.'

Blushing with pleasure at Joseph's regard for him, Kidney emptied the sugar into his cup.

In silence they waited for George to return. The lamp was guttering now, smoke staining the glass funnel. Moonlight lined the windowsills like a fall of snow.

There was a difference about the Monopoly game tonight. Whereas the night before George had appeared bored, hardly seeming to know what he was doing, now he proceeded skilfully to acquire the more expensive property. With his third throw he landed on Mayfair, then Park Lane. He studied the board intently and began to buy houses at £200 a time. It was his turn now to tell Joseph to throw the dice, to move three paces forward, to go to jail. It became a battle between the two of them. As they bought more property, their transactions with the bank took longer. May yawned and Lionel sat with his head bent low, a polite smile on his face, his hand inside the opening of his shirt.

In one such pause May said someone should go and look at Roland.

'Not now,' Joseph said. He was occupied in doing a swop with Balfour – Fleet Street for The Angel, Islington. 'Good, good,' he said triumphantly, paying his money and tucking the scarlet street card into his clip of property. He was astounded at May for buying two sites and not attempting to buy the third. 'You landed on it last go,' he shouted.

'Well, I didn't know,' May pouted. 'They all look alike to me.'

'But they're different colours, you nit.'

'Well, they still look the same to me.'

'Wild animals,' said Kidney, 'like mice or fleas, look extremely alike.'

'You mean each member of each species does,' amended George.

'Like the Arabs,' said Lionel, 'or the Chinese. Nothing to tell between them.' He got up from the table, excusing himself, and went towards the door.

'Go and look at Roland while you're at it,' his wife bade him, 'And make our bed ready for later.'

'We aren't sleeping in the barn,' said Lionel.

'I'm not going in the dark to that other hut.' May's voice was shrill.

Lionel came to her and stood with his hand on her shoulder. 'Shut your trap, May,' he said. He shook her a little, unplayfully, before releasing her.

It took Lionel some time to locate the candle and the matches on the washstand. There was a basin covering a jug alongside the saucer. He admired George and the MacFarleys. Everything as it should be. Roland looked very frail. Lionel inspected the lids of his shut eyes and the curved mouth, pale above the blankets and felt a stab of dislike. The child was like the father, a natural beast of the forest. He wished with all his heart that he hadn't told him about May and his coin. He

173

blew out the candle and took it back with him over the grass.

'Sleeping peacefully,' he announced, taking his place at the table.

He watched May secretly. Once he leaned forward to light her cigarette. She thanked him, bringing her face close to his held-out hand and he smelled her perfume and drew back severely into the shadows. What she had done, it seemed to him, was not in itself so dreadful. She had rendered him other little disservices during their married life. The deceits she practised were inspired by vanity, not by malice. He had, without her knowledge, forgiven her within himself on several occasions. But the cold hardening of the heart that he now experienced was totally strange, a prolapse of feeling that was beyond adjustment. He thought even his face was undergoing a change. He went to the sink and drank water, regarding himself in the mirror. It was his father's face that he saw reflected, the same righteous mouth, the similar unrelenting eyes gazing at him without understanding. He moved nearer the glass, saw the stubble on his cheek bone, the lobe of his ear looming large. He knew now who he was. What little remained of his old self felt a faint twinge of pity for that relation by marriage, his wife May, unaware of his transformation.

Not entirely unaware. She knew he had taken umbrage. She opened and shut her handbag several times. 'Have you a handkerchief, Lionel?' she cried at last. He didn't look up. She said desperately, 'Lionel, I'm talking to you.'

'Your move, I believe,' said Lionel, addressing Joseph.

The game continued. When May was declared bankrupt Joseph remembered Roland. 'Go and see him,' he told May.

May didn't care to admit she was afraid of the dark. She hovered on the top step of the porch and dabbed her foot into the field of moonlight like a girl by the sea. 'I don't know where the candle is,' she protested, coming indoors.

Lionel pointed at the saucer he had put on the draining board.

In the barn May didn't look at Roland's face. There were

174

too many shadows. She sat holding the candle on the far bed and began to count to a hundred. Perhaps she had been mistaken about the little boy and the pills. He was breathing quite normally. When she had counted to sixty she got up abruptly and ran back to the hut. The night was so calm the candle stayed alight. She entered the door with her face misty and the little flame intact.

'You look as if you'd seen a ghost,' said Joseph, looking up from his property cards.

'It's so creepy out there with that moon. It's different in the country.' She shivered affectedly. 'It looks – oh, I don't know – as if everyone had gone out.' She laughed at herself.

'Make some more tea, May,' ordered Joseph. She irritated him, wandering about, not doing anything constructive.

'Oooh,' wailed May, gazing helplessly about her. 'I've left my bag in the barn.'

'I'll go,' said Balfour, 'I'm out anyway.'

Joseph protested. 'You're not out, mate. You could mortgage those stations, you know.'

'Perhaps he's had enough,' George said, searching Balfour's face for signs of strain. 'Perhaps he should go to bed now.'

'I'm all right, George.' Balfour glanced apologetically at Joseph. 'I'll just go and fetch May's bag.'

'Please,' May said.

'See that Roland's covered up well,' shouted Joseph as Balfour left the hut carrying the candle. 'Make sure he's warm enough.'

As soon as he had finished this round he would go himself to look at the child, see he was warm and snug. He might even bring the boy inside to sleep in his bed if old Dot-Dot failed to return.

In the barn Balfour put down the candle and turned back the blankets on the iron bed. He felt Roland's forehead and his pulse. He drew the blankets high again and sat crouched on the bed holding the child's hand in his own. It wasn't his

175

child. He couldn't feel surprised or shocked. He had always, it seemed, been on the threshold of some experience that would open a door, and now here was just such an experience and there was no sudden illumination, no revelation such as he had imagined. Indeed it appeared to him that the door had closed for ever. He was quite untouched, it wasn't his loss. He thought perhaps he should be reacting differently. He should, like a man drowning, relive his gone-through life, but he couldn't do it. There were no pictures, no truths, no emotions. Soon, in a few hours, he knew there would be an ambulance and a general exodus, a dispersal into the landscape, a journey into another part of the wood. It would soon be over. He would go home and tell his Mam about it and she would cry out and he might just feel something then. Only because of her. Just as well. He was nothing really. There was no depth to him, no value. He put the little boy's hand under the blankets and stood up. 'Bye-bye,' he said, as if the child still lived, was dreaming still in the iron bed. He went out leaving the door open.

Outside he could hear the voice of May and then her laughter, as if she were happy. He looked at the roof of the hut cutting the August sky, and the moon, perfectly still, hung above the rise of the field. All the leaves on the trees glittered like glass.

Through the window he could see them grouped round the table – Lionel, May, George, Joseph. The lamp bloomed like a trapped and second moon.

When he entered, Joseph was telling Lionel to leave his money alone. 'Take your thieving hands off my lolly,' he shouted. He looked up. 'Everything all right, mate?' he asked full of fun, holding the paper money in his fist like a bouquet.

'No,' Balfour said. His head ached. 'He's d-dead.'